Jesus Is for Now!

JESUS IS FOR NOW!

Paul W. Powell

BROADMAN PRESS
Nashville, Tennessee

Scripture quotations marked (KJV) are from the King James Version of the Bible.
Unless otherwise noted, Scripture quotations are from the *New American Standard Bible*. Copyright © The Lockman Foundation, 1960, 1962, 1963, 1968, 1971, 1972, 1973, 1975, 1977. Used by permission.

"Got Any Rivers," page 105: Chorus copyright, 1945, "Youth For Christ Hymnal," Alfred B. Smith, owner. Verses copyright, 1946, in "Singspiration No. 4." Arr. Copyright, 1953, by Alfred B. Smith in "Sing Men No. 3."

"Before It's Too Late," Deanna Edwards from the album *A Song Is a Gentle Thing* by Deanna Edwards. Used by permission of Rock Canyon Publishers, 11514 Ventura Blvd., Suite A. Studio City, Calif. 91604 © 1980.

Library of Congress Cataloging in Publication Data

Powell, Paul W.
  Jesus is for now!

  1. Jesus Christ—Person and offices. I. Title.
BT202.P64 1985   232   85-4115
ISBN 0-8054-5006-8

To Mittie Heavin and Annie Lee Pool who knew me as a child, have loved me as a brother, and respected me as their pastor

Introduction

We live in a time of exploding change. People's lives are being torn apart, the existing social order is crumbling, and new life-styles seem to be emerging on the horizon. These changes are tearing our families apart, rocking our economy, paralyzing our political systems, shattering our values, and creating a new, often bizarre environment in which to work, play, marry, raise children, and retire.

All of this social, political, and economic change is mirrored in personal disintegration. Psychotherapists and gurus do a land-office business; people wander aimlessly amid competing therapies. They slip into cults and covens or, alternatively, into a pathological privatism convinced that reality is absurd, insane, or meaningless.

In all of this, I sometimes feel like the angel Gabriel in the play *Green Pastures.* Returning to heaven after being sent to earth to investigate the havoc of Noah's flood, Gabriel replied, "Lord, there ain't nothin' fastened down there anymore. Everythin' nailed down is comin' loose."

For a world where change is so profound that it challenges all of our old assumptions, old ways of thinking, old formulas, dogmas, and ideologies, I have good news! Jesus is the same yesterday, today, and forever. He is the solid Rock on which we can build a stable life. He is the secure Anchor who can steady us in the storms of change.

The best of the good news is this: Jesus is for now. The historical Christ is eternally revelant. He is not dead, and He is not gone. He is alive and He is here! When Jesus in the present tense is ignored, we live our lives in a spiritual vacuum. But when we magnify the present reality of the Christ, our faith assumes a new vitality.

The purpose of this book is to present the timeless Christ as the answer to today's severest problems. It is written with the conviction that He is both our Stabilizer and our Energizer.

Since Jesus is the Son of God, we ought to accept Him wholeheartedly, confess Him, serve Him, and imitate Him. We ought to give Him our supreme devotion. If these pages help to do that, they will have accomplished their purpose.

Contents

1

Living Life in Italics

Jesus lived His life in italics. No one else like Him has ever existed; no one more disciplined or dedicated or demanding, no one more consistent or creative or caring, no one more intriguing or infuriating or influential.

He was mild and gentle; yet when necessary, forcefulness pushed through humility. He could be both tough and tender. Jesus' life was a perfect blend of grace and gristle.

Beginning with a handful of diverse disciples, Jesus galvanized them into a church that literally turned the New Testament world upside down. At the age of thirty-three, He was crucified on a cross as a common criminal. In the end, this one man's self-sacrifice was the most potent force in defeating Rome, one of the greatest, most widespread empires in history.

The influence of Jesus is so prominent and dominant in history that we are compelled to ask: Who is Jesus?

People have always held one of three opinions about Him. The Pharisees believed that Jesus was possessed by the devil (Mark 3:22-3). The high priest accused Him of blasphemy (Mark 14:64). They believed that Jesus was a fraud, a liar. There are still people today who hold this opinion of Jesus.

At one time, Jesus' own friends believed that He had lost His senses (Mark 3:21). They knew that He was a good, sincere man, but they were afraid that the pressures of His ministry had become too much for Him and that He had lost touch with reality. Even His family tried to take Him back to the quietness of Nazareth, so He could escape the attention that they were afraid was having an adverse effect on Him (Mark 3:31-32). Some people today share this view of Jesus. They are sure that He was a good man but that He was definitely deluded about His identity.

And there were people like the Roman soldier who presided over the crucifixion of Jesus and recognized Jesus as the Son of God (Matt. 27:54). Likewise, millions of people today gladly and joyfully join him in the acclamation: Surely this is the Son of God.

This question, Who is Jesus? is the greatest question of time and eternity. If Jesus were a deceiver or if He were deluded, then we need to be forever through with Him. But if He is the Son of God, He is worthy of our greatest devotion and we ought to accept Him, confess Him, and follow Him joyfully.

As we try to find an answer to this question, we will look at four things about Jesus: His name, His aim, His claim, and His fame. These will help us to know who Jesus is.

What's in a Name?

First, consider the name of Jesus. The study of names has always fascinated me because names provide a clue to identity. Originally people had only one name. We read in history about men like Aristotle and Josephus. But Aristotle who? Josephus who? In ancient days, no one had a last name.

But as the population grew, it became necessary to add something to a person's name—a family association, an occupation, or a geographical location—to distinguish that person from others bearing the same name. So we read in the Bible about three Simons: "the Zealot," his political affiliation; "Simon a tanner," his occupation; and "Simon the leper," his physical affliction (Luke 6:15; Acts 9:43; Matt. 26:6).

Bit by bit, these identifying phrases evolved into the surnames of today. Names like Miller, Baker, Sawyer, and Smith originated in this manner.

The names of the Bible are rich in meaning. This is why we must consider the name of Jesus. When the angel announced the birth of Jesus to Mary, he said, "You shall call His name Jesus, for it is He who will save His people from their sins" (Matt. 1:21). The name *Jesus* is the same as the Old Testament name *Joshua,* which means "Jehovah is salvation." So we cannot even speak the name of Jesus without indicating who He is: He is the Savior of all people.

The unanimous testimony of Scripture is that in the name of Jesus the forgiveness of sins and salvation are offered to all people everywhere (Luke 24:47). The apostle Peter declared that there is no other name given under heaven whereby people must be saved (Acts 4:12). And the apostle Paul said that whosoever shall call on the name of the Lord shall be saved (Rom. 10:13).

Paul further emphasized the significance of Jesus' name when he told us how Jesus humbled Himself to the point that He was willing to give up heaven and come to earth as a man and die a criminal's death so that we could be saved. Then Paul declared:

> Therefore also God highly exalted Him, and bestowed on Him the name which is above every name, that at the name of Jesus every knee should bow, of those who are in heaven, and on earth, and under the earth, and that every tongue should confess that Jesus Christ is Lord, to the glory of God the Father (Phil. 2:9-11).

Because we find salvation through the wonderful name of Jesus, we often sing:

> Jesus is the sweetest name I know,
> And He's just the same as His lovely name,
> And that's the reason why I love Him so;
> Oh, Jesus is the sweetest name I know.

Shh, Don't Tell

Second, consider the aim of Jesus. Why did Jesus come to earth? What was Jesus' grand mission here? Did Jesus come to build a political or a military empire? No! When Jesus fed the multitudes, they were so moved by the miracle that they wanted to take Him by force and make Him their King. If He had come to be an earthly ruler, that would have been the time to inaugurate His kingdom and begin His reign. But Jesus dispersed the crowd and went on His way preaching and teaching (John 6:1-15).

Later Jesus taught His disciples that the mark of greatness in God's kingdom is not ruling over others but serving them. He summed up his ministry: "For even the Son of

Man did not come to be served, but to serve, and to give His life a ransom for many" (Mark 10:45). He did not come to reign; He came to redeem. He didn't come to be a king; He came to be our Savior.

Did Jesus come to be a miracle worker or a faith healer? Neither! The Gospels record forty-seven miracles He performed during His earthly ministry, but He performed them out of compassion, not for recognition. In fact, He often healed people and then said to them, "Shh, don't tell anybody" (see Mark 7:36). He did not want people following Him just because of His miracles.

Did Jesus come to gain wealth and material possessions for Himself? No! The apostle Paul declared that Jesus already had all the riches of heaven. Though He was rich, for our sake He became poor that we through His poverty might be rich (see 2 Cor. 8:9).

Why then did Jesus come? What was His aim? What was His central mission on earth? Paul summed it up for us in one completely reliable statement that all people should believe: "Christ Jesus came into the world to save sinners" (1 Tim. 1:15).

This is why Jesus was always pointing His disciples to the cross. He did not point them to His baptism when the Holy Spirit descended upon Him. He did not point them to the mount of transfiguration where the voice of God spoke about Him. He did not point them to His miracles which attracted the crowds to Him. He kept reminding them that He had to go to Jerusalem where He would be betrayed into the hands of sinful men, be crucified, and then be raised to life again on the third day (Mark 8:31; 9:31; 10:32-34). Jesus was a Man under orders. He was a Man on a

mission. He had come to the earth for the great purpose of
being our Redeemer—our Savior. Both His name and His
aim help us to know who Jesus is: the Son of God and the
Savior of the world.

He Verified His Claim

Third, listen to the claim of Jesus. It is consistent with
both Jesus' name and His aim. Jesus asserted, "He who has
seen Me has seen the Father" (John 14:9). Again He said,
"I and the Father are one" (John 10:30). And when He was
on trial before Pilate, He was asked, "Are You the King of
the Jews?" Jesus answered, "It is as you say" (Mark 15:2).
The real force of Jesus' answer has been lost in its transla-
tion from the Greek to the English. Jesus answered literally,
"Yes, emphatically so! You said it! I am the Son of God."
In all of these statements, Jesus was making the same great
claim that He was the Messiah, God's Son.

Jesus made many other claims that were consistent with
this number-one claim. For example, Jesus claimed to have
power to forgive sins. Did He? Can such a claim be substan-
tiated? Yes! On one occasion a man who had been crippled
from birth was brought to Jesus. Jesus said to the man,
"Son, thy sins be forgiven thee" (V. 5, KJV). That caused
eyebrows to be raised in the crowd listening to Jesus that
day. The people knew that only God has the power to
forgive sins. Was Jesus claiming to be God? Jesus read their
minds and their lips. He knew that they doubted His power
to forgive sins. How could He convince them that He had
such a power? There was one way to do it. He asked,
"Which is easier to say, 'your sins be forgiven or 'arise and
walk'?"

While the people knew that only God could forgive sins, they also knew that only God could heal a crippled man. So Jesus declared, "But in order that you may know that the Son of Man has authority on earth to forgive sins," He said to the paralytic, "I say to you, rise, take up your pallet and go home" (Mark 2:1-11). The man got up and walked. The man's healing verified the claim of Jesus that He was able to forgive sins.

Jesus claimed to have all authority in heaven and in earth. Did He have that kind of authority? Yes. He spoke to the winds, and the winds ceased blowing. He spoke to the seas, and the seas became calm. He spoke to demons, and the demons fled from Him. He spoke to the diseased, and they were cured. All things in heaven and earth obeyed the command of Jesus (Matt. 8:27).

Jesus claimed to know the future. But did He? Yes. He discerned that one of His disciples had a devil in him, and Judas did (John 6:70). He prophesied that Simon Peter would deny Him three times. And although Peter did not believe he would ever do such a thing, he did. Peter came to realize what we all need to face: Jesus knows us better than we know ourselves (Matt. 26:31-35). Jesus stated that the shepherd would be smitten and the sheep would scatter. The night of His arrest, His disciples fled into the night and deserted Him as He had said they would. He knew all things then, and He still knows all things.

Jesus comforted Martha with, "I am the resurrection and the life; he who believes in Me shall live even if he dies" (John 11:25). He did not say, "I have come to tell you about the resurrection." Nor did He say, "I have come to point you to the resurrection." What Jesus did say was: "I am the resurrection. Was he? Did He have the power to raise the dead? He went to the grave of His friend Lazarus who had been dead for four days and, standing outside, Jesus called out, "Lazarus, come forth" (v. 43). And Lazarus came out of the grave alive. Jesus never met a funeral possession that He didn't break up by raising the dead. I believe that, if Jesus had not called Lazarus by name that day, all the dead of all the ages would have come out of their graves.

Jesus said, "I, if I be lifted up from the earth, will draw all men to Myself" (John 12:32). For two thousand years now, the cross has been the magnet of history. People from all nations, all cultures, all races, and all languages have been drawn to the crucified Christ to find both abundant life and everlasting life in Him.

Jesus said, "I am the door" (John 10:7). Through Him men have found a ready access to God. Jesus said, "I am the light of the world" (John 8:12); wherever He and His message have gone, the darkness of superstition and ignorance have been dispelled. Jesus said, "I am the bread of life" (John 6:35), and He gives the water of life; when people have taken Him into their lives, they have had their hunger and thirst for God satisfied. Jesus said, "I am the vine" (John 15:5); when people have come to Him, they have found a vital, living relationship with God. Jesus said, "I am the good shepherd" (John 10:11); And those who have followed Him have found guidance, care, and leadership for all of their lives in Him. All of these, along with His name and His aim, help us to know who Jesus is: the divine Son of God and our Savior.

The Message of History

Finally, look at the fame of Jesus. It is popular today for historians to pick at the scabs of great people, exposing their flaws and inconsistencies. But the longer and more closely people look at the life of Jesus the more sterling His character shines. Historian Kenneth Scott Latourette reminds us, "As the centuries pass, the evidence is accumulating that, measured by his effect on history, Jesus is the most influential life ever lived on this planet." "And," he said, "that influence appears to be mounting."

With most people just the opposite is true. Their influence diminishes with their deaths and with the passing of time. Sometimes I hear people compare men like Mahatma Gandhi to Jesus, presuming Jesus to be only one of many saints. Their mistake is confusing God with Godlikeness.

The book *Mahatma Gandhi and His Apostles* by Vedmethta reveals some interesting things, among them that the Gandhi influence thirty years after his death has waned. This is true despite the fact that Gandhi's followers recorded every word he said and despite the fact that four hundred books have been written about him. According to the author, Gandhi's disciples have scattered. They have found inspiration in new masters and in new causes. The point is that Gandhi was a great man; Jesus was God.

Put these all together—the name of Jesus, the aim of Jesus, the claim of Jesus, and the fame of Jesus—and they help us to know who Jesus really is. Who is Jesus? The centurion was right. He is more than a man. He was and is the Son of God and our Savior. Since this is so, we ought to accept Him, confess Him, and follow Him as our Lord.

2

A Purpose for Being

Thinkers everywhere agree that one of the most dominant needs of all people is meaning in life—a purpose for being. As James Gardner observed, "Man is a stubborn seeker of meaning."

One of the reasons Jesus' life exuded such confidence and authority was: He knew who He was, why He was here, and where He was going. His confidence lay cemented in the knowledge that His purpose was always to do the will of the Father.

He expressed that will, that purpose, that mission on earth when He announced:

> The Spirit of the Lord is upon me, because he hath anointed me to preach the gospel to the poor; he hath sent me to heal the brokenhearted, to preach deliverance to the captives, and the recovering of sight to the blind, to set at liberty them that are bruised, To preach the acceptable year of the Lord (Luke 4:18-19, KJV).

The occasion for that statement was Jesus' first visit to His hometown of Nazareth after He had begun His public ministry. His fame as a preacher and miracle worker had spread rapidly. He was back for a visit to the town where He had grown up. As was His custom, He went to the synagogue to worship on the sabbath day. He was already a noted teacher and a preacher, and He asked to read the Scriptures and to deliver the sermon that day. So He took the scroll of the prophet Isaiah, turned to what we know as Isaiah 61:1-2, and read it to the congregation. This passage is a prophecy concerning the Messiah. When Jesus had finished reading this prophecy, He said to the congregation, "Today this Scripture has been fulfilled in your hearing." Jesus declared to them that He was the Messiah whom Isaiah had predicted. He was the Savior for whom they had longed. This passage from Isaiah tells us most clearly why Jesus came.

There are five reasons for Jesus' coming. He came for consolation—"to heal the brokenhearted." He came for emancipation—"to preach deliverance to the captives." He came for illumination—to restore "sight to the blind." He came for liberation—"to set at liberty them that are bruised." And He came for salvation—to announce that redemption was now available and to fulfill His role as Redeemer.

In these five words—*consolation, emancipation, illumination, liberation,* and *salvation*—we have an answer to why Jesus came initially. They also tell us what He can and will do for us today if we will follow Him.

Why did Jesus come? What was His overriding mission on earth?

Give Him All the Pieces

Jesus came first of all for consolation: He came to heal the brokenhearted. Brokenhearted people are all about us. Broken hearts aren't restricted to any one class or race of people. I doubt if you could find a single pew in any church or a single home in any community that does not have at least one broken heart in it. A loved one—husband, wife, child, or a parent—has been lost in death. A marriage or a career has not worked out. A child has gone astray, and the dreams and hopes for that child have been shattered. An illness, a disease, or some physical defect has come. Something has happened to almost every one of us at some time, leaving us with a broken heart.

What can we offer to all of these people with broken hearts? When they come to us distressed about their families, their health, their children, their marriages, what can we say to them? Are we to say: "I am sorry for you, my friend. Jesus can save you from your sins, but He can do nothing about your broken heart. You must go elsewhere to find help for that." Must we say to people that Jesus is good for the "sweet by and by" but He can do nothing for the "nasty here and now"? No, we have a message for the brokenhearted people of the world.

John Gary, a retired minister friend, told me that when he was a boy he saw a sign in a blacksmith's shop which read: "We can mend anything but a broken heart and the break of day." Then he said, "Thank God, I know someone who can mend even a broken heart." So do I.

If a person with a broken arm came to me seeking help, I would say to him, "Go to a physician, and he will help you." And if a person with a broken heart comes to me, I can say to him, "Go to Jesus, the Great Physician. He can heal your broken heart." That's a part of why Jesus came. Listen to Jesus' invitation to the brokenhearted:

Come to Me, all who are weary and heavy-laden, and I will give you rest. Take My yoke upon you, and learn from Me for I am gentle and humble in heart; and you shall find rest for your souls. For My yoke is easy, and My load is light (Matt. 11:28-30).

If you are sad, if you are dejected, if you are depressed, come to Jesus today. It is amazing what He can do with a broken heart if you will give Him all the pieces.

A Soul in Chains

Jesus also came for emancipation: He came "to preach deliverance to the captives." These captives are not people in jail. They are people under the bondage of sin. As Jesus said, "Everyone who commits sin is the slave of sin" (John 8:34).

William Penn once wrote, "Men must be governed by God, or they will be ruled by tyrants." Penn was speaking politically, but his statement is also true spiritually. Lust is a tyrant. Greed is a tyrant. Superstition is a tyrant. Anger is a tyrant. Ambition is a tyrant. Sin is the tyrant that rules over people apart from Christ.

We all know that the drunkard becomes a slave to alcohol and that the drug addict becomes hooked on drugs. But the perfectionist can become so in love with details that he becomes cruel and irritable with those who have not attained a love for completeness. And the housekeeper can love for her house to be tidy—so tidy that she is unhappy when people relax and are at home in it.

Everywhere people have bad habits that they can't seem to break. They want to be free from these things, and they have said a thousand times that they are going to change, but they never do.

Herodotus, the historian, recorded that the Persian king, Darius, once sprained his foot while out hunting. He retained at his court the most distinguished members of the Egyptian medical profession. Their treatments, however, only aggravated the condition of his foot. The king spent seven sleepless days and nights. Finally, someone told him of a certain Democedes of Croton who had unusual medical skill. Democedes at this time was a slave. He was brought into the king's presence, trailing chains and clad in rags. Democedes was able to soothe the king's foot and promote its healing. As a reward, Darius gave Democedes two pairs of golden fetters.

Sin is like that. It leads eventually to bondage. Sometimes its chains are of iron, and sometimes they are of gold, but the same enslavement results. The only difference is the price of the chains.

People have always known their sin without having the ability to do anything about it. But Jesus can set us free from the bondage of sin. We no longer need to live in slavery to Satan and wrongdoing. We can be free persons. We can know liberty in Jesus Christ. That is one of the reasons He came.

Spiritual Glaucoma

Jesus came also for illumination: He came to give "sight to the blind."

There are two kinds of blindness in the Bible: physical blindness (a blindness of the eyes) and spiritual blindness (blindness of the soul). Handel, after he had written *The Messiah,* went blind. But he said, "I believe that my ability to see Christ increased as my ability to see others decreased."

Jesus did restore the sight of many people who were physically blind, but He came primarily to give sight to those who were spiritually blind. Because of Christ's coming, many people have seen themselves and God and eternity and others for the first time.

It is possible for a person to have poor vision and not know it. That happened to me. When I was in college, I was having a difficult time seeing the blackboard. I thought that it was just because of a glare from the window. I thought maybe everybody was having the same problem I was. Then one day I was at a southwest conference baseball game when a friend made a comment to me about something that was written on the center field fence. I asked, "Can you read that sign?" He said, "Sure I can. Can't you?" I said, "I can't read a word of it." He said, "Man, you must be blind." So I went to an optometrist, and, sure enough, I needed glasses. I had a vision problem, and I didn't even know it.

Many people today are in that same condition spiritually. They do not see their own sinfulness. They have never caught a glimpse of the glory of God. They have no vision of eternity. They grope in spiritual darkness, blinded by Satan, the god of this world. But Jesus can open our eyes to spiritual reality (John 8:12). If we come to Him, He can give sight to the blind. That's a part of why He came.

Light and Liberty

Jesus also came for liberation: He came "to set at liberty" those who "are bruised." The "bruised" are the oppressed or downtrodden. Oppression is much deeper than slavery. It carries with it a sense of being crushed, defeated, and whipped down by life.

Many people are not only bound by their habits but are also crushed by their emotions, attitudes, and outlooks. They need to be liberated from fear and worry, from depression and loneliness, from pessimism and doubt as well as from their sinful appetites.

Ernest Hemingway, one of the most celebrated writers ever to pick up a pen, said, "I live in a vacuum that is as lonely as a radio tube when the batteries are dead and there is no current to plug into." Then he put a shotgun to his head and pulled the trigger.

A young lady who had just gone through a divorce came to me for counseling. She said, "Since Bill didn't want me, I just decided that nobody wanted me." That kind of loneliness and despair, meaninglessness, and misery crushes people everywhere. Jesus came for such oppressed people. He came to help us overcome our inferior feelings, our bad attitudes, and our negative outlooks.

A few weeks ago I was in Rio de Janeiro, Brazil. If you are ever there, one of the sights you will want to see is the huge statue of Christ that overlooks the city of Rio. It is called "Christ the Redeemer." The Christ of stone stands on a high mountain with hands outstretched to welcome all who come to the city. As I stood looking at that massive statue, I remembered the words of some unknown poet who wrote:

> The Christ of my land
> is cement and sand,
> Who cannot see or hear or feel
> the miseries of my people.
> The Christ of my land
> is cement and sand.

Then I thought, *Hallelujah! The Christ of the Bible is alive, alert, and active. He sees and hears and feels the hurts of all people.* He can deliver those who are downtrodden. The one who holds the stars in heaven also reaches down to lift us up when life comes crushing in upon us.

With People It Is Impossible

We dare not miss the last of the reasons Jesus came. He came also for salvation: He came "to preach the acceptable year of the Lord." Jesus came to announce that the day of salvation has come. God's offer, God's promise, God's provision is now available. Receive it today. Salvation can be yours.

If Christ had not come to die for our sin, we would not have had a chance to be saved. But because He came, all people can be saved. A rich young man once came to Jesus asking, "What shall I do to obtain eternal life?" When Jesus told him what to do, he felt that the price was too high. He turned and sorrowfully walked away. Then Jesus said to His disciples, "How hard it is for those who are wealthy to enter the kingdom of God!" (Luke 18:18-24). Jesus wasn't belittling riches. He was just warning us that riches tend to make a person feel self-sufficient and independent, and those feelings make it hard for a person to pray: "God be merciful to me a sinner." Unless people come to this place of humility, repentance, and faith, they cannot be saved. That's why it is so hard for wealthy people to be saved.

That surprised Jesus' disciples. They believed that riches were a sign of God's favor. They said, "If rich people have a hard time being saved, then who can be saved?" (see Luke 18:26).

Listen to Jesus' answer. It is vital to us: "The things impossible with men are possible with God" (v. 27). No one is good enough to merit salvation. No one is rich enough to buy salvation. And no one is strong enough to earn salvation. Our only hope is to receive it as a gift of God's grace. To be saved, we must admit that we are sinners and that we are helplessly and hopelessly lost. Then we must rely on, trust in, and adhere to Jesus Christ as Savior.

Because Jesus came, redemption is now available to all. We need only to turn to Him in repentance and faith.

Why did Jesus come? He came to heal the brokenhearted, to set the captives free, to give sight to the blind, to give liberty to the downtrodden, and to be our Savior. If you have a broken heart, come to Jesus. If you are gripped by unbreakable habits, come to Jesus. If you are bound and blinded by a negative outlook or a bad attitude, come to Jesus. If you are oppressed and depressed by life, come to Jesus. If you are lost and want to be saved, come to Jesus. He came for you.

3

It's Sink or Swim

When it comes to the crucial issues of life, we must either swim with Jesus or sink in despair. He is the only adequate answer to the major problems that confront us. When faced with the dilemma of continuing to follow Christ or departing from Him with the multitudes, we say, with Simon Peter: "Lord, to whom shall we go? You have words of eternal life. And we have believed and have come to know that You are the Holy One of God" (John 6:68-69).

The occasion that led to Simon Peter's conclusion and confession was Jesus' feeding of five-thousand men with just five loaves of bread and two small fish. By that deliberate miracle, Jesus gave a sign to the people that He was fully able to satisfy all of their needs by Himself.

However, the multitudes missed the real meaning of the miracle and wanted to take Jesus by force and make Him their king simply because He had fed them. This was not what Jesus wanted, so He dispersed the crowd and crossed the Sea of Galilee to the other side.

The crowd, however, followed Him to the other side of the lake, so He rebuked them for wanting only a "bread-

and-butter" preacher. Then He urged them to seek the
Bread of life rather than mere physical bread.

This Bread of life intrigued the crowd, and they asked
Him to give them some of this "bread." Jesus told them
that He was the Bread of life Himself and that those who
came to Him would have their spiritual hunger fully satisfied (John 6:35).

Building on this analogy, Jesus insisted that people must
eat His flesh and drink His blood in order to have eternal
life.

This shocked most of His listeners, and they found it too
difficult to accept. So many of them turned and went away
from Jesus. At this point, Jesus asked His twelve remaining
disciples, "Will ye also go away?" Peter answered, "Lord,
to whom shall we go? thou hast the words of eternal life"
(John 6:67-68, KJV).

To whom shall we go today? With the crucial issues of
life, the deepest problems of life, and the greatest needs of
life, where shall we go? To whom shall we go with our
broken hearts? With our broken lives? With our broken
homes? Or with our broken world? There is ultimately only
one Person to whom we can go: Jesus. He alone is adequate
for all situations, all crises, and all times. He alone is a Man
for all seasons.

Broken Hearts

Jesus is the only adequate answer for our broken hearts.
The world had hardly begun when it was drenched with the
tears of sorrow. The Book of Genesis contains only two
chapters of bliss and then begins its tale of woe. Adam and
Eve sinned, Cain slew his brother Abel. From these experi-

ences flows a trail of blood and tears that continues throughout the pages of the Bible, the pages of history, and right onto the pages of today's newspaper. All around us are people whose hearts are broken in sorrow.

Who can comfort us, heal us, and help us in our hours of grief? Listen to the offer of Jesus:

> Let not your heart be troubled: ye believe in God, believe also in me. In my Father's house are many mansions: if it were not so, I would have told you. I go to prepare a place for you. And if I go and prepare a place for you, I will come again, and receive you unto myself; that where I am, there ye may be also (John 14:1-3, KJV).

John Bunyan's *The Pilgrim's Progress* is one of the greatest books ever written. The two pilgrims, Christian and Hopeful, received a summons to the Celestial City and at one point came to the River of Death. When they saw how deep and wide and swift and dark its waters were, they were stunned. They met two men whose raiment shown like gold and whose faces were as the light. The pilgrims asked the men if there were another way to get to the gate of the heavenly city. Were there no boats? No bridges? No ferries? One man said, "There is no other way except through the river." Then they asked the man, "How deep is it?" The angel answered, and this is almost the greatest thing in all the book, "You shall find it deeper or shallower as you believe in the king of the palace."

Christian and Hopeful stepped into the water. When they did, Christian began to sink. He cried out to his companion, "I sink in deep waters: the billows go over my head; all the waves go over me."

But Hopeful answered, "Be of good cheer, my brother: I feel the bottom, and it is good."

With that, Christian broke out with a loud voice, "Oh, I see him again; and he tells me, 'When thou passest through the water, I will be with thee; and through the rivers, they shall not overflow thee.'" Then he took courage and crossed safely over the river.

There is an old song that expresses our hope in the hour of sorrow and death. Its words go like this:

> I won't have to cross Jordan alone,
>   Jesus died for my sins to atone;
> When the darkness I see,
>   He'll be waiting for me,
> I won't have to cross Jordan alone.

Jesus, the Savior, is the only One who can give us comfort during life and hope after death. If we will come to Him, He will help us in our hour of sorrow and grief (Heb. 4:14-16).

Broken Lives

Jesus is the only adequate answer for our broken lives. Melville's novel *Moby Dick* is a classic tale of Captain Ahab, who had a feud going with a great white whale of the deep. The captain had already lost his leg in an encounter with the great white whale and had become a brooding, unhappy, sullen, and terribly pessimistic man. Most of the time he kept himself closed up in his cabin.

On one of those rare occasions when he was walking around the deck of his ship, he came upon the ship's blacksmith, who was working on some metal. Captain Ahab said to him, "What are you doing, Smithy?" And he replied, "I am knocking the dents out of the harpoon, Captain." Captain Ahab stood there for a moment, then pointed to his heart and said, "Smithy, do you know anything that will take the dents out of here?"

We begin our lives in the innocence of childhood, but it is not long until we are marred and scarred by the blows of a thousand sins. We start out thinking we can break the Ten Commandments only to discover that they break us. When that happens, what can we do? Where can we go to straighten out the dents of our hearts and to mend our broken lives?

Jesus is the only Person I know who can help. If your life has been broken by sin, I have good news for you. The carpenter of Nazareth still mends broken men and women.

William Muehl told years ago the story of a five-year-old who had worked all fall on a ceramic dish that he wanted to give his parents for Christmas. On the last day before the holidays, after the traditional Christmas program, the lad was trying to run down the hall, put on his coat, and wave good-bye to all at the same time. In the process, he slipped down and crushed the carefully wrapped package with a terrible breaking noise. There was a moment of silence; then when the child realized what had happened, he broke into uncontrollable sobs.

In an effort to comfort him, the father said, "Don't cry, Son, don't cry. It really doesn't make any difference." But the mother, far wiser in things like this, brushed him aside and said, "But it does matter; it matters a great deal." Then she swept up the child in her arms and wept with him. When that had passed, she stooped over gently and said,

"Let's pick up the pieces and see what we can make out of what is left."

That's what Jesus keeps saying to you and me: Bring me the pieces of your broken life, and together we shall make something of what is left.

Broken Homes

Jesus is the only adequate answer for our broken homes. Marriage and family are fighting for their lives in contemporary America. The divorce rate in America doubled between 1970 and 1980. And the number of divorces among middle-aged people has jumped 80 percent in the past decade while the population growth for that age group increased only 4 percent over the same period. It seems to me that we are rapidly coming to the place where a happily married couple is an oddity.

Overall, 51 percent of American marriages now end in divorce. For every marriage that dies with a formal funeral called divorce, others die and are never legally declared dead. They are living deaths held together by children, economic necessity, social pressure, or religious convictions. This means that we can drive down the streets of any of our major cities and know that in every other house people are facing a major domestic problem.

Where can we go for help with our broken homes? Who is adequate to enter into our marriage relationships and salvage them? What can hold our marriages together today? It is not a marriage license. That is only a legal document. It can be nullified as easily as it was ratified. It is not a wedding ring. That is only a metallic symbol that can be taken off as easily as it was put on. And it is not a wedding ceremony. That is only a social custom. Christ can best hold a marriage together. I almost never encounter an experience of marital failure in a home where Christianity is a vital factor. Most marriage problems arise because of our selfishness, pride, and just plain meanness. Having Christ in our lives takes a great deal of the abrasiveness out of our personalities and helps us become more loving, considerate, and sensitive mates. And that's what makes for good marriages.

At the outset of His earthly ministry, Jesus was invited to a wedding in Cana of Galilee. During the reception that followed, the host ran out of refreshments. Wedding receptions in those days were not forty-five-minute affairs tacked on to the end of the wedding. They lasted for several days and were characterized by feasting and great celebrating. To run out of refreshments would prove terribly embarrassing to the host and to the bride and groom.

Jesus' mother intervened. She told Jesus of the problem and instructed the servants, "Do whatever He tells you" (see John 2:5). Jesus told the servants to fill the large clay waterpots. When they had done this, He told them to draw some of it out and take it to the person in charge. The steward, not knowing its source, tasted the water-now-turned-to-wine and said, "You have kept the best till now!" (see John 2:1-11).

Transforming the molecular contents of the liquid was only one of the miracles of that day. Turning failure into success was another. As that marriage would have been marred from the beginning without His intervention, so many homes are marred in the end because He is not allowed to enter.

Mary's words to the servants are our cue to a happy marriage! "Do what He tells you!" Invite Jesus into your life, obey His every command, and you will find the greatest help possible for your marriage and your home.

Broken World

Jesus is the only adequate answer for our broken world. People have always dreamed of a better world. They have longed for a Utopia where there will be no war, no poverty, no hate, no disease, and no crime. Every time scientists go into laboratories to find a cure for cancer, they are dreaming of a world where there will be no more disease. Every time social workers go into the slums to work with the poor, they are dreaming of a world where there will be no more poverty. Every time politicians sit down at conference tables to try to negotiate peace, they are dreaming of a world where there will be no more war. However, war, poverty, hate, disease, ignorance, and crime are still great burning social problems. To whom shall we go for an answer to war? To whom shall we go for an answer to hatred and racial prejudices? To whom shall we go for help with all of the great social issues of today?

Shall we go to science? No! Science has made the world a neighborhood, but it cannot make the world a brotherhood. Science has enabled us to walk safely on the moon, but we still can't walk safely on our own streets. Science has enabled us to make tremendous technological strides, but it has not solved the basic moral and spiritual problems of people.

Shall we go to education? No! Higher education does not change our lower nature. Knowing all about biology does not make persons more sensitive to the loneliness of those around them. What good is there in knowing a foreign language if we cannot say a kind word in our native language? If education can solve our basic problems, why do students have to lock their cars on campus and why do professors have to watch students to keep them from cheating? And why must we have police officers at our athletic contests?

Shall we go to the politicians? No! Some people say that what we need is more and better laws. But I have never pastored in a city where the chief law enforcement official did not either confess to a crime or become indicted for some crime. It is not unusual today for a politician to be featured in *Time* one week and be "doing time" the next. What we need is not more and better laws. We need fewer and better lawmakers.

Shall we go to more religion? No! The world has long been filled with religion. And we recognize that there is some good in all religions: Hinduism, Buddhism, Shintoism, Confucianism, and Judaism. However, religion has not changed the world.

To borrow a phrase from Paul Rees: "Nothing can save a tottering civilization but a towering Savior."

Abraham Lincoln once observed, "I have often been driven to my knees by the realization that I had no other place to go." That's precisely the predicament we find ourselves in today. That's why I say, in the face of the great issues of life, we must either swim with Jesus or sink into despair. Where else is there to go? He alone has the answers to our greatest needs. He alone is adequate for every circumstance of life. He is a God for all seasons.

4

Go and Sin No More

Dr. Horace Williams, who was for many years professor of philosophy at the University of North Carolina, once commented, "When I found out Jesus was not a Methodist, it was a shock. And then I discovered He wasn't even an American!"

Many people would probably be shocked to know what Jesus is really like. We all tend to make Him like we are: Anglo-Saxon, Protestant, American—and in my part of the country, a Texan—and even a Southern Baptist.

But the more I know about Jesus, the more I realize that He is different from all of our sectarian labels. One passage that reveals this is Jesus' experience with the woman taken in adultery (John 8:1-11).

One day, as Jesus was teaching in the Temple, He was interrupted by the scribes and Pharisees, the watchdogs of religious orthodoxy. They had caught a woman in the very act of adultery and had brought her to Jesus for judgment.

Their question to Jesus was this: "Now Moses in the law commanded us, that such should be stoned: but what sayest thou?" (v. 5, KJV). The scribes and Pharisees were enemies of Christ and had long been looking for a good way to discredit Him publicly. This seemed to be the perfect one. From a purely legal point of view, the scribes and Pharisees were correct. The law of Moses *did* require that a person guilty of adultery be stoned to death (Deut. 22:23-24). The woman was clearly guilty. Their accusations were not a matter of hearsay. They had actually caught her in bed with a man.

But this law of Moses had fallen into disuse at that time. Besides, the Romans who had conquered Israel forbade the Jews from inflicting capital punishment without the sanction of the Roman ruler. The Romans certainly did not hold adultery as grounds for capital punishment, so they would not have sanctioned the stoning of the woman for such an offense. Now, you can see the dilemma.

If Jesus said, "Stone her," He would be going contrary to the law of Caesar. If He said, "Forgive her," He would be going contrary to the law of Moses. If He said, "Condemn her," He would be branded as a rebel. If He said, "Pardon her," He would be branded as a heretic. How could He win? What could He say? Any answer He gave would be wrong.

Jesus understood the motives of the scribes and Pharisees, so He refused to dignify and satisfy them with an answer. Instead He stooped down and began to write on the ground and said nothing.

But the Pharisees would not leave Jesus alone. They were determined to have an answer. They kept on asking Him: "What do you say? What is your opinion?" Finally, Jesus spoke. He answered in essence, "OK, you want an answer: stone her! But let the one among you who is without sin cast the first stone." Then Jesus stooped down and began to write on the ground again. Between what He said and what He wrote, a change took place. The silence of the circle was broken by the thud of stones falling in the sand. What did He write? We will never know, but it produced conviction and compassion, and when He looked up, all of the woman's accusers had gone. He alone was left with the her.

Then Jesus asked of her, "Woman, where are those thine accusers? hath no man condemned thee?" She replied, "No man, Lord." Then Jesus said to her, "Neither do I condemn thee: go, and sin no more" (vv. 10-11, KJV).

The importance of this experience is that it reveals how the top management in the head office of heaven deals with sin and with sinners. It also teaches us the different ways we ourselves can deal with sinners. We can employ Moses' way and condemn the sinner to be punished. We can use the Pharisees' way and expose and embarrass them publicly. Or we use the Master's way and forgive them.

Sin must be reckoned with. The woman was caught in her sin, and we can be sure that our sins will find us out also (Num. 32:23). Either in time or in eternity or in conscience, our sins will eventually find us out. Sometimes they find us out swiftly, as in the case of Ananias and Sapphira. Sometimes they find us out slowly, as in the case of David. But be sure of this: One day our sins will catch up with us.

The Scriptures remind us, "He that covereth his sins shall not prosper: but whoso confesseth and forsaketh them shall have mercy" (Prov. 28:13, KJV). We all have the same choice: We can cover our sins, or we can confess them. If we choose to cover our sins, we will not prosper. If we choose to confess them and forsake them, we will receive pardon. The Lord will either deal with our sins in mercy now or He will deal with them in judgment later. The choice is ours.

The best thing, the only wise thing, for us to do then is to bring our sins to Jesus now and let Him deal with them as He dealt with that woman. The way Jesus dealt with her then is how He deals with sin and sinners today.

The three statements Jesus made to the woman show how He deals with sinners. His first statement, "Woman, where are thine accusers? hath no man condemned thee?" shows His compassion. His second statement, "Neither do I condemn thee," reveals His consistency. His third statement, "Go, and sin no more," shows His candidness (John 8:10-11).

If the world shall last for a million years, this experience and these three statements will stand as a testimony to all the world about how God treats sinners and also about how we should treat them.

Jesus Is Compassionate

The way Jesus first addressed the woman shows the greatest of tenderness and compassion. He said, "Woman, where are those thine accusers? hath no man condemned thee?"

Notice that Jesus addressed her simply, "Woman." He could have called her a lot of other things. He could have called her a prostitute, a harlot, or something worse. After all, name calling is one of the main ways we sinners have of judging, condemning, and belittling other sinners. But He didn't do that, and He wasn't a sinner either. He addressed her simply "Woman."

Woman is the same word He used to address His own mother at Cana and from the cross. At the wedding in Cana of Galilee, the host ran out of wine at the wedding reception. Mary intervened and told the servants to do whatever Jesus commanded them. Jesus responded, "Woman, what do I have to do with you? My hour has not yet come" (John 2:4). And from the cross, as He committed the care of His mother to John the beloved apostle, He said, "Woman, behold your son!" (John 19:26). Whenever the word *woman* fell from the lips of Jesus, it was always spoken in infinite tenderness and compassion. We can be sure of that.

The woman responded to Jesus' question by saying that all her accusers were gone and there was no one left to condemn her. Jesus had made sure there were no accusers by saying earlier, "He that is without sin among you, let him first cast a stone at her" (John 8:7, KJV). In that statement, our Lord revealed for all times that the only people qualified to condemn others for sins are those who are completely sinless. That statement put me out of the stone-throwing business for the rest of my life. Like the scribes and the Pharisees in this story, I have disqualified myself.

John's way of describing what happened to this woman's accusers is marvelous. He said, "And they . . . being convicted by their own conscience, went out one by one, beginning at the eldest, even unto the last" (v. 9, KJV). I like to think that the oldest one left first because he was the wisest. Age often mellows, and experience broadens. The cocksureness of youth gives way to a more loving heart and a mind that is slower to judge and quicker to understand.

As Goethe said, "One needs only to grow older to

become gentler in one's judgments. I see no fault committed which I could have not committed myself."

When George Whitefield saw a criminal on the way to the
gallows, he uttered the famous sentence, "There, but for
the grace of God, go I." I have lived long enough to know
that there is within my heart the potential to do any evil that
has ever been done. There are thoughts and desires in all
of us that would shame hell itself at times. Like those
scribes and Pharisees, we may not have done what they
were accusing the woman of doing, but we have thought
about it, and we have wanted to. And by our own conscience we are accused and condemned.

On my desk is a rock that I purchased on a visit to the
Dead Sea several years ago. Inscribed on it are these words
of Jesus, "Let him who is without sin cast the first stone."
I keep it there to remind me to be compassionate with
people who have fallen into sin. No matter what people tell
me, they know that I will pray for them, weep with them,
and give them advice; but I will not throw rocks at them.
I am just not qualified.

We need to guard at all costs against a critical, condemning, judgmental spirit that makes us more like the scribes
and Pharisees than like Jesus. We not only are not qualified
to judge others but also we libel ourselves when we do so.
We will be judged by God as we judge others (Matt. 7:1;
Rom. 2:1). If anything ought to encourage us to be compassionate with others, it ought to be that fact.

I am forever amazed and alarmed at how insensitive and
calloused and critical and how unlike Christ some religious
people can be. We should strive to become like Jesus and
deal compassionately with other people. The only folk who

have a right to condemn others are those who are sinless themselves.

Jesus Is Consistent

Jesus' second statement to the woman shows His consistency in dealing with sinners. He said, "Neither do I condemn thee" (v. 11, KJV). That statement is in keeping with His whole mission. He did not come for condemnation but for redemption.

He said to Nicodemus, "For God so loved the world, that he gave his only begotten Son, that whosoever believeth in him should not perish, but have everlasting life. For God sent not his Son into the world to condemn the world; but that the world though him might be saved" (John 3:16-17, KJV).

Jesus' very purpose for coming into the world was not to judge it but to redeem it. In keeping with that purpose, that mission on earth, Jesus said to the woman, "Neither do I condemn thee."

He was the only one present that day who had the right to condemn her, and He chose not to. He chose to forgive her. She deserved justice, but she needed mercy. Jesus always offers us what we need, not what we deserve.

A lady went to a photographer once to have her picture made. When she went back to view the proofs, she was upset. She said to the man, "I don't like these pictures. They don't do me justice." The photographer replied, "Lady, you don't need justice; you need mercy."

That's the way it is with all of us. We really don't want justice. We want mercy. If the Lord should mark iniquities, who among us could stand? Jesus came for our salvation,

Obviously, Jesus believed that he could help the sinner become a saint. Jesus' method was not to condemn but to inspire.

So when we come to God—the one against whom we have ultimately sinned—He does not condemn us nor condone our sin but rather calls us to a higher life. He is willing to give us a second chance even though we do not deserve it. He says to us, "You have made a mess of things, but your life is not finished. I am giving you another chance."

He challenges: "You can yet become what you were created to be. This does not have to be the end. Your life is not over yet. Get up, and get on with living as I want you to." And He says that with such authority that we know that He will enable us to live above the life we have known before.

I wonder what happened to the woman after her encounter with Jesus. No one knows for sure, but I have an idea. Her answer to Jesus' question, "Where are your accusers?" gives us a hint. She said, "No man, Lord" (v. 11, KJV). The fact that she addressed Him as Lord is evidence that she recognized who He was and that she believed in Him. My guess is that this woman was truly repentant and that she opened her heart to the One who loved her for what she could become not for what she was. And she accepted His offer of a new life.

I think in that moment, face-to-face with Jesus, she became painfully aware of her sin, committed herself to Him, and walked away a new person. That's the way Jesus dealt with sin and sinners then, and that's the way He deals with them today.

A captive was once brought before James II of England.

The king chided the prisoner, "You know that it is in my power to pardon you?" The trembling captive replied, "Yes, I know it is in your power to pardon me, but it is not in your nature."

It is both in the power and the nature of Jesus to forgive and to pardon. The fact is that none need ever go away from Him unforgiven. He has paid the price for our sins. He will forgive us. This experience teaches us that it is in both His power and His nature to do so.

5

Here Comes the Bridegroom

Joy is one of the dominant notes of the New Testament. It is tragic that so little of it is felt or expressed in most modern churches and by most Christians. I have attended many churches and heard excellent sermons badly delivered. The whole service lacked cheerfulness. The tone of the minister's voice and his inflection were all depressing. This is almost the worst of faults in any preacher. Faith and hope and love are cheerful and should be preached in that manner. Life is not always bright, but Christianity ought to be.

If the world could see in us a little more happiness and a little less gloom, a little less judgment and a little more compassion, it would be more attracted to Jesus because He was an immensely happy person.

Jesus described His work and His relationship to the world as that of a bridegroom. We have often heard Jesus called the Good Shepherd who came to seek and to save the lost sheep of the world. And we have heard Jesus called the Great Physician who came to make people whole. But not nearly enough attention has been to Jesus as the Bridegroom of the church.

Jesus gave us this image of Himself when He was being questioned by the Pharisees about fasting. They wanted to know why Jesus' disciples did not fast and practice the kind of asceticism that John the Baptist practiced. Jesus replied, "You cannot make the attendants of the bridegroom fast while the bridegroom is with them, can you? But the days will come; and when the bridegroom is taken away from them, then they will fast in those days" (Luke 5:33-35).

Jesus' use of the image of a bridegroom suggests both the purpose and the nature of His ministry. As the Bridegroom of the church, He is the lover of humanity who has come to woo and win us to God. And as the Bridegroom, He and His followers were immensely happy.

John the Baptist was a preacher of judgment. There was more fire and brimstone per square inch in John's preaching than in anyone else I know. He was a somber, austere man who lived life close to the bone. He both preached and practiced fasting. To fast is to do without food for an extended period of time as an act of religious devotion. It is the practice of self-denial for a spiritual purpose. If you have ever been on a diet, then you know that doing without food is no fun. John the Baptist was a "no fun" kind of man.

But Jesus was not like that. He made it clear that His disciples did not fast because they were not sad. Feasting, not fasting, was more characteristic of Jesus' life and His movement. To make fasting a part of His ministry would be like putting a new patch on an old garment: it would be out of place.

Remember that Jesus compared Himself to a bridegroom, not a funeral director. Therefore, our worship services ought to be more like a wedding than a wake. And as

His followers, we ought to look and act more like wedding attendants than like pallbearers.

I'm afraid that most modern Christians have taken on more of the spirit and attitude of John the Baptist than that of Jesus. Many people look upon the church as nothing but a collection of colorless religious creeps who come to worship services and sit with blank stares on their faces while they listen to irrelevant sermons. And in many instances this is true. A lot of Christians go to ball games and yell like fans; but at church, they sit like statues. A lot of worship services begin at eleven o'clock sharp and end at twelve o'clock dull.

I have attended some worship services where I felt like the little boy who attended church for the first time. On the wall there was a memorial plaque that had been placed there in memory of the congregation's young men who had given their lives in the military service of their country. The little boy became captivated by that plaque. In the middle of the worship service, he leaned over and asked his mother, "Mother, what's that for?" Thinking that an answer might keep him quiet for the rest of the service, the mother answered, "Son, that has been placed there in memory of the boys who died in the service." The little boy then asked, "Mother, which service did they die in—the morning service or the evening service?"

This kind of lifelessness and joylessness in many churches may have stimulated the famous remark about Christianity by Friedrich Nietzsche, a German philosopher: "If you want me to believe in your Redeemer, you'll have to look a lot more redeemed."

Jesus never counted it a sin to be happy. He was happy

Himself, and He wants us to be also. What a challenge the joy of Jesus is to us today to let that note sound loud and clear in both our private lives and our public worship. The world has enough sadness of its own without our adding to it.

Luke told of the deep joy of Jesus when he wrote, "At that very time He rejoiced greatly in the Holy Spirit" (Luke 10:21). The occasion of this statement was a return of the seventy from their preaching mission. Jesus had sent out seventy others in addition to His twelve apostles on a tour of the nearby cities and towns. He had given them specific instructions for going and working. They went gladly according to His divine command. And, after a time, the seventy came back and gave a glowing account of their work.

They were all filled with joy at the tremendous success of their first large-scale evangelistic tour under the command of Jesus. And when they told Him that even the devils were subject unto them in His name, Jesus, as if in musing, said, "I was watching Satan fall from heaven like lightning" (v. 18). Then the text goes on to say, "At that very time He rejoiced greatly in the Holy Spirit."

The verb *rejoiced* is a very strong word. It means that Jesus was ecstatic. He showed rapturous joy. The same word used here is also employed to describe the joy Mary felt as she told her cousin Elizabeth that she was going to give birth to the Savior (Luke 1:47). It is the same word that is used to describe the joy the Philippian jailer felt when he was converted to Christ (Acts 16:34). And it is the same word that is used to describe the joy that will be in heaven at the marriage supper of the Lamb (Rev. 19:7).

The use of this particular word and everything in this whole paragraph shows that at this moment Jesus had the joy of Christmas, the joy of salvation, and the joy of heaven all at the same time. Jesus was indeed a joyful man. His life was characterized by triumphant, ecstatic, rapturous joy.

What caused Jesus to rejoice in this hour? What led to this happy experience? If we can learn the answer to these questions from this passage, it will help us to know what we may do to bring joy to Him today. To know the answers to these questions will teach us the source of much joy in our own Christian experience.

Three things caused Jesus to experience and express ecstatic joy on this occasion. In the success of the seventy, He saw the fall of Satan, the ministry of His saints, and the salvation of sinners. When He saw these three things, He rejoiced in the Holy Spirit.

The Defeat of Satan

The seventy returned from their preaching mission saying, "Lord, even the demons are subject to us in Your name" (v. 17). At that time Jesus said to them, "I was watching Satan fall from heaven like lightning." The demons represent Satan's power on earth. In their defeat, Jesus saw the final defeat of Satan and the ultimate triumph of the gospel. He saw in the preaching of the seventy the power of Satan broken. He saw this as an evidence of the sudden, complete, and decisive defeat of the devil.

Satan is the archenemy of God and God's people. He is our accuser and our adversary. He is constantly at work seeking whom he may destroy (1 Pet. 5:8). Sin entered the world when Adam and Eve yielded to the temptation of

Satan in the Garden of Eden. At that time he became the god of this world, and he has had tremendous sway over it ever since. But even in the Garden, God promised redemption. He said to Satan: "I will put enmity/Between you and the woman,/And between your seed and her seed;/He shall bruise you on the head,/And you shall bruise him on the heel" (Gen. 3:15). On the cross, Jesus was bruised by the power of sin and Satan. But on the cross, the ultimate defeat of Satan was accomplished. Paul therefore declared, "The God of peace will soon crush Satan under your feet" (Rom. 16:20).

As the disciples gave their report, Jesus remembered the prophecy of God, anticipated the coming crucifixion, and saw that through their preaching of the good news the final defeat of Satan would be accomplished. The battle would be won. The victory was assured. So Jesus rejoiced in the Holy Spirit.

Every time the gospel is preached, the boundaries of the kingdom of darkness are driven back. Every time we tell the good news, we hasten the full and final defeat of Satan. This is what caused Jesus to rejoice then, and it is what causes Him to rejoice now.

The Ministry of the Saints

Second, Jesus rejoiced in the ministry of His saints. Hitherto, only the twelve apostles were at work. Now, seventy others were working. These seventy were all laypersons, plain-vanilla Christians. They were sent out two by two on this great mission for the Lord just as the apostles had been sent. Up until now it seems that only the twelve had been given the power and the responsibility for witnessing. The rest of Christ's followers were but spectators, observers of the work. Now he broadened the base to include all followers. Now the average layperson was involved in the great missionary effort to reach these cities of Christ. When Jesus saw this, He rejoiced.

This kind of vast missionary and evangelistic involvement always causes our Lord to rejoice. The divine plan of Jesus is that all of His disciples should be witnesses. The layperson is as much called to be a witness for Christ as is the preacher. Every saved soul is an ambassador for Christ. The ideal of the kingdom of Jesus is that every man and woman, everyone saved by His grace, shall be a personal herald and witness for Jesus Christ.

Our Lord rejoiced on this occasion because He beheld that day a prophetic vision of the victories that would come to His church down through the ages. He knew that preachers and laypersons, working together, would go forth with the life-giving message of the gospel of the redeemed love which is centered in Him, the Savior of the world. Jesus rejoiced with unspeakable joy as He beheld that vision.

Have you ever noticed that the really important figures in the New Testament are not priests and monks, but shepherds, fishermen, tax collectors, soldiers, politicians, tent makers, physicians, and carpenters? On the shoulders of such people, the gospel went forward and the church was built.

Elton Trueblood was right when he said that the only kind of church that can crack the modern world is one in which every member is a missionary. There are thousands of missionary tasks, and each must find his own. Oh that we might come to this blessed and glorious ideal of our Savior!

Christianity is not merely a badge to be worn. Salvation is not simply a thing to be possessed. It imposes a solemn obligation upon every one of us to put forth our best efforts to win the lost to Christ Jesus the Savior. Our Lord rejoiced on this occasion because His people were measuring up to His divine plan.

We can add to the rejoicing of the heart of Jesus, as well as to that of our own heart, if we will become personal witnesses and evangelists and supporters of world missions. Serving Christ and obeying Him bring to us the greatest joy in all the earth. One of the reasons the note of joy is so absent from many Christians' hearts is that they are not involved in Christ's service.

Jesus, however, quickly cautioned His disciples not to rejoice because the demons were subject unto them. They should rejoice because their names were recorded in heaven. In other words, rejoice in what you are, not in what you do. Our success-crazed world needs this warning.

We must be careful not to exaggerate the importance of the deeds we accomplish. When our joy and success are marked by doing rather than being, we often become jealous, competitive, and deceptive.

We must not find our joy in our momentary successes alone, for the time may come when we will not be successful. Then where will our joy be? Our joy must not be in our momentary victories but rather in our eternal relationship. The fact that we are saved and secure and our names are written in heaven brings us our greatest joy. Therefore, when we go out witnessing and working for Christ and we aren't successful, we shouldn't feel that we are failures. Our relationship with Christ is still secure.

Not our victories but God's ultimate sovereignty over evil is the ground of our hope and the basis of our rejoicing.

The Salvation of Sinners

After hearing the report of the missionaries, Jesus then offered a prayer of thanksgiving to God. He said, "I praise Thee, O Father, Lord of heaven and earth, that Thou didst hide these things from the wise and intelligent, and didst reveal them to babes" (Luke 10:21).

Jesus rejoiced because His work of redemption was reaching out to all people. The "wise and intelligent" were the scribes and the men who were schooled in the traditions of their religion. They were people who had arrogantly depended on their own intellectual capacities to understand all things. They had become so proud in their learning that they were blind to the simple truth of God. The "babes" were the humble folk, the ordinary people, who without arrogance or pretense were receptive to God's revelation of Himself in Jesus. Thus they responded to and were receptive to God's word. The truth of God in Christ is revealed truth. It does not require earthly knowledge but heavenly grace to understand it.

One of the dangers of education is pride in one's self and one's powers. We can become so accustomed to analyzing, scrutinizing, and classifying information that we exclude any vision of things in their concreteness, wholeness, and simplicity. It is quite possible to be so clever and so learned that in the end we cannot see the forest for the trees. In short, we can become educated beyond our intelligence; we can become too smart for our own good.

True wisdom is always humble and in a certain sense

naive. This is especially true when it comes to the revelation of God. After all, we must always remember that Christianity does not mean knowing all of the theories about the
New Testament; still less does it mean knowing all of the
theories about Christ because Christianity does not mean
knowing about Christ; it means knowing Christ.

Do not misunderstand me. No premium is to be placed
on ignorance by Christians. When we come to church, we
don't unscrew our heads and leave them outside the door.
We are to love God with our minds as well as our hearts and
our spirits. Nonetheless, the truth of God in Christ is revealed truth and only those who are willing and able hum-
bly to receive a revelation can know it.

Wherever and whenever Jesus sees common people re-
sponding to the gospel and being saved, His heart leaps
with joy. The Bible declares to us that there is joy even in
the presence of the angels of God over one sinner who
comes to repentance (Luke 15:10). Jesus knows no greater
joy than seeing another come to Him as Lord and Savior,
and neither should we.

Jesus then is the Bridegroom of the church. He came to
woo us and win us to the Heavenly Father. If we respond
to His love and His proposal with a glad and joyous "I do,"
we can know His joy also.

6

Back to Jesus or the Jungle

The do-your-own-thing philosophy in America is about to do us in today. Our emphasis upon individual freedom and personal rights has gone from the sublime to the ridiculous. The crime rate is soaring; vandalism and violence are spiraling; the breakdown of marriage and the disintegration of the home is staggering; corruption in government and the betrayal of trust in public office are shameful; and the use and the abuse of drugs, including alcohol, is shocking. Every kind of evil—including promiscuous sexual behavior, venereal disease, and abortion—is increasing.

We have come to such a time of moral and spiritual confusion that many people do not know right from wrong. They are not even sure that there is such a thing as right and wrong.

Even our churches have caught this spirit of the age. There are many proponents of what has been called "religion a la carte." They pick and choose only the part of the menu that suits their liking; that is, they believe only the parts of the Bible that they want to believe, what moral standards they want to hear, what part of Christ's mission they will support, what form of devotion they will practice, and what they will believe about God.

The only absolute that many people recognize is absolute freedom, and we ought to know that absolute freedom is absolute nonsense. We are so constituted that we need authority in every area of life. In society, we need government. In the home, we need parents. And in the moral and spiritual realm, we need God. Ultimately, all authority stems from Him. Right is right because God said so. Wrong is wrong because God said so.

God has ordained government (Rom. 13:1). God tells us to honor our fathers and mothers (Ex. 20:12). God is our final authority in all moral and spiritual matters.

The reason we are suffering such moral, spiritual, and social decay in our country is that we have cut ourselves off from God. As a flower cut from its roots will soon wither and die, so we are a cut-flower civilization. You can't have fruit without roots. If we want the fruit of law and order in society, truth and honesty in government, security and stability in the home, we must return to the roots of our faith and trust in God.

A final court of appeal for settling all moral and spiritual questions is necessary to avoid hopeless confusion. If there is no authority in life, we must each decide ourselves, each for oneself, what is right and what is wrong. As finite beings, we must act as if we were infinite; since that is impossible, we are driven into complete insecurity, anxiety, and despair.

Ultimately, the supreme authority for our lives is the person of Jesus Christ, speaking through the infallible record of God's inspired revelation. We must recognize, acknowledge, and accept the authority of Jesus Christ over our lives if we want to bring order out of chaos.

Those who are spiritually perceptive always recognize Jesus' unique authority. Luke tells us about one such man. He was a Roman centurion who had a servant who was near death. Feeling himself unworthy to approach Jesus personally, he sent a delegation to ask Jesus to heal his servant. Jesus responded by going to the man's house. When the centurion saw Jesus coming from a distance, he sent another delegation to tell Him that he did not feel worthy of Jesus' coming under his roof. He felt that all Jesus needed to do was to speak a word and his servant would be healed (Luke 7:1-10). That man had a marvelous understanding of the truth. He believed that Christ had complete and unlimited authority. He said in essence, "Lord, You don't have to come to my house. You can heal my servant long distance."

Then he said, "For indeed, I am a man under authority, with soldiers under me; and I say to one, 'Go!' and he goes; and to another, "Come!' and he comes; and to my slave, 'Do this!' and he does it" (v. 8). The centurion recognized that just as he had authority vested in him by Rome, so Jesus had authority vested in Him by God. He needed only to speak and things would be done.

Since Jesus is vested with the authority of God, He has the right to tell us what to believe and how to live today. He has the right to direct our lives and our churches. He is the supreme authority for all creation. Since Jesus has the authority of heaven, obedience to Him is not optional but obligatory. The authority of Jesus is a challenge to all of us today to bow before Him as Lord and to follow Him without reservation.

While the authority of Jesus is complete, there are three areas of life in particular where the authority of Jesus needs to be recognized. Jesus has authority to correct, authority to cleanse, and the authority to command.

The Authority to Correct

In every area of life, the secular as well as the spiritual, we need and must have an authority to avoid endless confusion.

Greenwich mean time is the international universal time standard. By it, all clocks are ultimately set. Can you imagine what would happen if suddenly Moscow insisted that their central clock was standard? Then London would protest and say Big Ben was the irreducible right time, and America would probably go by the wristwatch of the president of the United States. Without a standard there would be international pandemonium. The world must agree on one single, nondebatable fixed reference point for time-keeping.

In similar fashion, ships at sea in the northern hemisphere have their nondebatable point of reference: the North Star. And musicians worldwide always come back to concert *A* as their agreed upon standard. Concert *A* is always 440 vibrations per second. Can you imagine the disharmony in music if there were no international standards?

Just so, in matters of faith and practice, we must also have an authority. We have that authority in Jesus Christ.

By virtue of who He is, Jesus and His teachings are authoritative for our lives today. God has not left us to grope in a moral and spiritual fog not knowing what to believe or how to live. He has not set us adrift on uncharted seas without a compass. He has given us the sure word of His Son to guide us in these matters. His teachings are fixed constellations by which we may eternally guide our lives.

When Jesus taught during His earthly ministry, He didn't talk as if He had simply read the book; He talked as if He had written it. In the Sermon on the Mount, He said repeatedly, "You have heard that it was said . . . But I say to you . . ."

He didn't preface His teaching with "thus saith the Lord" as the prophets did. And He didn't footnote His sermons with quotations from ancient scholars as the scribes and Pharisees did. He relied on no external credentials. Thus He made His words equal in authority to God's law.

Today, we must return to Jesus' teachings as the authority for our lives. It's either back to Jesus or back to the jungle. If we don't return to Jesus and instead continue on our present course of moral and spiritual decline, we will soon have to change our national symbol from an eagle to a vulture.

The Authority to Cleanse

Not only did Jesus teach with authority but He also acted with authority. During the last week of Jesus' life, He made His triumphal entry into the city of Jerusalem. There He allowed the people to acclaim Him as God's anointed: the Messiah. When He went to the Temple, He saw that it had been diverted from God's original purpose. Instead of being a place of prayer, it had become a place of merchandising.

The Temple was the focal point of worship and symbol-
ized the whole Jewish religious system. The fact that it was
being grossly misused indicated the perversion of the
whole religious establishment of that day. There were two
things that particularly distressed Jesus.

First, there was the business of moneychanging. Every
Jew had to pay a Temple tax of one-half shekel near the
Passover time. For general purposes, all kinds of currency
were equally valid in Palestine. But this tax had to be paid
in a special coin of high grade silver. The function of the
moneychangers was to change the unsuitable currency into
the correct currency. The problem was that they charged
an exorbitant rate to make the exchange, the equivalent of
one fourth to one half day's pay for a working man. This
whole thing lent itself to abuse and exploitation of the
people who had come to worship, and no doubt the moneychangers made a large profit.

The selling of animals for sacrifices was worse. For most
visitors to the Temple, some kind of offering was necessary.
One of the most common offerings was doves. It was easy
enough to find animals for sacrifice outside the Temple.
But any animal offered in sacrifice had to be without blem-
ish. Officials inspected the animals, and most likely they
would reject any animal bought outside the Temple and
would direct the worshiper to the Temple stalls and
booths. The problem was that prices inside were almost
double that of outside prices. This was an abuse. Some of
the stalls were even owned by the high priest. So, the Temple became a place of trading and exploitation of the poor
and the humble pilgrims.

Thus the religious leaders squeezed the worshipers for

every penny they could get out of them. The result was that the Temple grounds had become a place of buying and selling, bickering and dickering, bargaining and arguing with so much noise and confusion that the person who genuinely wanted to meet God would find it almost impossible to do so. When Jesus saw these abuses, He was angered; and in disgust, He turned over the moneychangers' tables and drove those who sold animals out of the Temple. He cleansed the Temple to restore God's house to its original purpose.

The religious leaders of that day wanted to know by what right Jesus did what He did. He told them through questions and parables that His authority came from the same place as that of John the Baptist—heaven (Matt. 21:23-27).

As John was from God, so Jesus was from God. As John's voice was God's voice, so Jesus' voice was God's voice. Their authority came from the same source.

Jesus had a right to do what He did. He had a right to establish the purpose of God's house and to remove anything that perverted that purpose. Jesus is not only the Lord of the individual, He is also the Lord of the church. People, councils, committees, and boards may think that the church is theirs to control, but unless Christ's authority is recognized in the church, God's will never be realized through the church.

What is the purpose of God's house? Is it just a place where religious hucksters preside over the baptism of babies, perform weddings, and conduct funerals? Is it, as somebody has said, just a "hatching, matching, and dispatching society"? Jesus tells us the church's purpose. He said, "It is written, 'My house shall be called a house of prayer.' " Jesus' intent is that the church be a place where people can meet God.

John Claypool tells that several years ago he was driving through North Carolina and came upon a lovely little country church nestled in a cove. The sign out front read, "Mount Carmel Baptist Church, founded—1796." And underneath were the words "Where men meet God."

I submit to you that this is what the church ought to be—a place where God and people meet together. This is what worship is all about—God and people getting together.

Worship is always a spiritual experience. It is that experience that quickens the conscience by the presence of God, keeps the mind on the truth of God, purges the imagination with the beauty of God, and opens the heart to the will of God.

There is nothing quite like walking into a house of God knowing that He will be there. Whatever distracts or takes away from meeting God does not belong in the church.

Authority to Command

After the resurrection Jesus met with the disciples and said:

> All authority has been given to Me in heaven and on earth. Go therefore and make disciples of all the nations, baptizing them in the name of the Father and the Son and the Holy Spirit, teaching them to observe all that I commanded you; and lo, I am with you always, even to the end of the age (Matt. 28:19-20).

These were the last words of our Commander in chief.

They represent what ought to be the highest priority of every believer's life. There seems always to be a running battle between those who believe in the priority of evangelism and those who believe in the priority of discipleship. Each tends to emphasize one to the neglect of the other. But on the authority of Jesus, we are to do both. We are to busy ourselves at making, marking, and maturing disciples until He comes again.

Charles Schulz, the creator of the comic strip *Peanuts,* is a lay preacher. He decided some years ago that one of the greatest ways to convey spiritual truths was through a comic strip. If you are a faithful reader of *Peanuts,* you know how the thrust of a spiritual message can suddenly come breaking through the pages to your heart. One of the comic strips tells of a hot day in August when Charlie Brown and his baseball team were playing a most important game. Everything seemed to be going against them. Nobody hit the ball. The first time they took the field Lucy, out in short center field, saw a pop fly coming right toward her and just stood there. The ball fell to the ground not a foot in front of her.

That was too much for Charlie Brown. He threw his glove down on the mound, and he walked out past second base to center field and began to read her the riot act. On and on he went. He finally said, "What in the world were you doing?" Lucy had stood with a blank kind of stare on her face while Charlie Brown spoke. When he finally finished, she said with a very pious voice, "I was having my quiet time."

The moral of the story is this: there is a time to pray, and there is a time to play ball. There is a time to worship, and

there is a time to work. There is a time to seek God, and
there is a time to seek people. Jesus commanded us to do
both.

In 1872 William Carey read the mandate in Mark 16:15,
"Go ye into all the world, and preach the gospel" (KJV).
"Lord," he said, "do you mean William Carey?"

As he pondered that verse he said, "Yes, Lord, you must
mean William Carey, and I will respond. I will go and
preach the gospel."

The Lord not only meant William Carey but also means
you and me. He commands every one of us to go and
preach the gospel.

Jesus has the right, the authority, to tell us what to do.
He tells us this plainly in the Great Commission. Now we
must either do it or be guilty of insubordination to our
Commander in chief. The authority of Jesus must either be
absolute or obsolete. He is either Lord of all, or He is not
Lord at all. If we are as spiritually perceptive as was the
Roman centurion, we will recognize Jesus' authority readily, accept it completely, and submit to it joyfully. To do so
is to recognize Jesus as Lord and Master of all of life.

7

Jesus Didn't Back Away

According to heart specialist Dr. George Sheehan, the weakest among us can participate in athletics, but only the strongest can survive as spectators. When you are a spectator, the wrong things go up and the wrong things come down. Body weight, blood pressure, heart beat, cholesterol, and triglycerides go up; vital capacity, oxygen consumption, flexibility, stamina, and strength go down.

Being an onlooker in the arena of Christian living can also be risky. The wrong things go up and the wrong things come down. When you are a spectator Christian, criticism, discouragement, disillusionment, and boredom go up. Sensitivity to sin, human need, God's resources, and the Word of God go down. The most deadly thing that can happen to our churches today is to fill them with indifferent and uninvolved members. There are to be no born-again, blood-bought, heaven-bound, spectators in the army of Jesus Christ. Inactivity and uninvolvement are subversives of the worst sort.

There is an example of the kind of involvement we all need in the experience of Jesus' cleansing of the Temple. At the outset of His public ministry, Jesus went to Jerusalem to observe the Passover. When He arrived at the Temple, He saw the moneychangers and the selling of the animals such as I described earlier. The mercenary motive of these semi-legal blackmailers desecrated the Temple in Jesus' eyes. In addition to their dishonesty, there was so much haggling, bargaining, and transacting of business that one would have a difficult time praying if one wanted to. Reverence fled the hearts of worshipers who had been met with injustice instead of solemnity. Prayer could not grow out of an emotion of resentment, and worshipers could not have a deep sense of God's presence under such circumstances. The outer courts of the Temple, which were the only places the Gentiles could enter, had become more like a stockyard than places of prayer. How could even the most sincere seekers worship amid such confusion and deception?

Being familiar, these practices became legitimate. No one thought anything about them until Jesus felt a flash of zeal for the sanctity of His Father's house. Jesus, picking up some cords of rope that had been used for cattle and sheep, plaited a whip and advanced on the whole crowd and drove them from the place of worship.

Jesus saw the courts, the place where men and women drew night unto God, desecrated and could not remain silent. Jesus' cleansing of the Temple was a bold and daring act of deep significance for several reasons.

First, by it He was declaring Himself to be the Messiah predicted in the Old Testament (Mal. 3:3).

Second, it showed what an amazing man Jesus was. To separate a group of schemers from their spoils and do it alone shows what a forceful spirit and dynamic personality

Jesus had. But most of all it revealed his burning enthusiasm. That was what impressed His disciples most. At
first they were shocked at this revolutionary onslaught
against the ecclesiastical status quo. Never before had they
seen Jesus in this vigorous role. Such strenuous acts by
Jesus needed justification and explanation. He had dared to
challenge the most sacred institution in Jewish life. Out of
a burning passion for the true purpose of the Temple, He
had taken a bold and revolutionary step. Jesus' disciples
were driven to the Scriptures for an explanation. They
remembered that it was written of the Messiah: "Zeal for
Thy house has consumed me" (Ps. 69:9). The word *consume*
means "to devour, to burn hot within." The psalmist saw
the Messiah as having a concern, a zeal for God's work that
would motivate Him to action. It would not allow Him to
stand idly by and see injustice and wrong taking place. He
would be compelled to act. That's what Jesus' disciples saw
in Him that day as He cleansed the Temple. The enthusiasm that Jesus showed is a challenge to us today. It is
the kind of enthusiasm that ought to characterize all of
God's people.

The idea of enthusiasm scares some Christians. They
pride themselves in being cool, stoical, and unemotional.
They associate enthusiasm with wild-eyed fanatics. Enthusiasm, however, is not a shallow emotion; it is a deep
commitment that causes us to be willing to get involved, to
act, to risk for the cause we believe in.

The greatest danger we face as Christians is not that we
shall become fanatical, but that we will become lukewarm,
insipid, and indifferent. The danger is that we shall be

content to be spectators instead of participants. We will not care enough to get involved.

Involvement is risky. When Jesus cleansed the Temple, it cost Him His popularity immediately and it cost Him His life later on. But He was so deeply committed to God and God's will that He could not see what was going on, stand idly by, and not get involved.

Those of us who are committed to Jesus Christ ought to be the most involved, enthusiastic, committed, and excited people on earth. If we want God's work to go forward in a great way, we must be enthusiastic about it. We must have enough burning zeal to get involved, to risk, to take the offensive.

Our zeal for God and His work ought to point in four directions. It ought to lead us to do four important and meaningful things: to attend the church, to commend the church, to extend the church, and to defend the church.

Attend the Church

This whole experience happened while Jesus was in the place of worship. Jesus, you know, made a habit of attending worship regularly, and we should also develop that habit in our lives. The Scriptures admonish us not to neglect meeting together as the people of God for regular worship (Heb. 10:25).

Why do we need to attend church? There are four good reasons. We go to church for education—to be taught, to learn; we go to church for inspiration—to be motivated; we go to church for association—to make Christian friends; and we go to church for cooperation—to do together for God those things which we cannot do by ourselves.

Every Christian ought to work for God individually. We ought to do what we can for Christ by ourselves. But there are some things we can only do together as a group. For example, we can evangelize our own neighborhoods by ourselves, but we cannot evangelize the world by ourselves. We Christians have a responsibility to do both. So we band ourselves together in churches to carry out the Great Commission of our Savior.

With many people, church attendance is largely a matter of habit, but so are many other matters in our lives. Of course, I hope our readers attend church out of a higher motive—commitment to Christ. Bad habits regarding health care are dangerous. The same goes for our faith. We do not break church membership vows; they break us! The faithful readily exclaim, "I was glad when they said unto me, 'Let us go into the house of the Lord'" (Ps. 122:1).

Commend the Church

By the lives we live, by the words we speak, by the ministry we render, we are continually commending or condemning the church of Jesus Christ to other people.

The church today has many critics. Some continually accuse it of being filled with hypocrites. But we are under no illusions about ourselves. We make no false claims as to what we are. We are not perfect; we are only forgiven. However, as we seek to follow the Savior, we must, by the lives we live and the deeds that we do as well as the words that we speak, commend Him to a lost and dying world.

In his autobiography, the Duke of Windsor told of his early life as the Prince of Wales and his renunication of the throne of England. He said that his father, the king, often remonstrated him with, "Remember your position and who you are." In other words, his behavior was to be consistent with his identity as the child of the king. The same should be true of us. Lloyd Perry says that the world has become so "churchy" and the church has become so worldly that one can scarcely tell the difference between the two. We cannot commend the church to others unless we live the gospel that we claim to preach.

Extend the Church

It is no accident that this incident we are talking about took place in the court of the Gentiles. There were four courts for worship in the Temple. The central place of the Temple included the holy place and the holy of holies. Surrounding the holy place and the holy of holies was the court of the priests, where only the priests worshiped. No one else was allowed inside that court. Outside the court of the priests was the court of the Israelites where the men of Israel worshiped. No woman was allowed inside that court. Beyond the court of the Israelites and surrounding it was the court of women where Jewish women went to worship. Beyond that was the outer court of the Temple, the court of the Gentiles where non-Jews, people from foreign nations, could worship. In this area reserved for a response to God by other races, trade had usurped the place of worship and business had been substituted for worldwide compassion. Such behavior showed the state of the heart of the Jewish people.

They had forgotten that their true mission on earth was to be a nation of priests for the whole world. They had become proud, nationalistic, and exclusive. They thought only of themselves and of the ease and comfort of their own worship. Gentiles! What do Gentiles matter? Certainly use their court and desecrate it. This was the supreme indignity to the heart of Jesus, so He swept out the whole unholy traffic. If they were going to continue to make the house of God a privileged sanctuary of nationalistic exclusiveness instead of an open center for worldwide evangelism, they deserved the judgment of God upon them. And that's what they got. Jesus intended that God's work be extended to all people everywhere.

The house of God must ever and always be open to all people for whom Christ died. We ask no one: What education do you have? How much money do you have? What position do you hold? What profession are you in? We invite little children to come and grow. We invite the uneducated to come and learn. We invite the weak to come and be strengthened, and we invite the lost to come and be saved.

Where else in the world is there such an organization as the church? There are those who say, Let the rich come. There are others who say, Let the professionals come. And there are still others who say, Let the educated come. But where else are people told: Whosoever thirsts, let him come and drink of the water of life freely?

The church is to work and labor to extend the kingdom of God to all people everywhere.

Defend the Church

The burning passion of Jesus was to defend God's house against perversion. It was to keep the Temple for God's intended purpose—a place of worship for all nations. Sig-

nificantly the only time Christ ever used force in His ministry was not to drive sinful people to the Temple but to drive
profane people out of it.

We must ever give ourselves to defending the church of
God against creeping perversion and keep it at God's intended purpose. Someone has said that erosion is not as
fast as explosion but that the end results are just as devastating. It is easy to neglect the house of God until its original
purpose is eroded and people are no longer meeting God
there. We tend to drift, almost imperceptibly, from the
course God has drawn out for us. History is littered with
denominations that have ceased to preach and teach the
Bible and now are on the dust heap of time. They are no
longer vital forces for God. The same thing can happen to
us.

So let the church stay always at its intended task. Let the
church be more than a mausoleum for the living dead. Let
the church be more than a nursery for overfed and over-
pampered spiritual infants. Let the church be more than an
insurance agency for the spiritually desperate. Let the
church be more than a country club catering to the spiritually elite. Let it always be a pillar, not a pillow, of truth
where people can meet God and know Him vitally. We
must always be at the task of defending the church as Jesus
did.

We must ever be on guard against the frostbite of indifference. The world does not need to have a monopoly on
enthusiasm. Unless we Christians care enough to get involved, to risk, to act, we will never make a mark for God.
Jesus was enthusiastic, and His attitude should challenge us
to be enthusiastic also.

8

Jesus Loves Me, This I Know

Several years ago Karl Barth, the world-renowned theologian, made his first visit to the United States. Following his speech in the chapel at Union Seminary, Barth met with a group of students and faculty members for an informal dialogue. During the discussion one of the students asked, "Dr. Barth, you have spent your lifetime studying and teaching the Bible, and you know many things. Can you sum up your vast theological findings for us in just a few sentences? Can you in a few words share with us what you believe to be the heart of the Christian faith?"

Barth, who at that time was an old man, settled back in his chair, lit his pipe, and for a moment disappeared in a cloud of smoke like Moses on Mount Sinai. When the smoke cleared, Barth said, "Yes, I think I can sum up what I believe in a few short sentences."

Then he answered the astonished young students in words familiar to most preschool children, "It is this: Jesus loves me! This I know, For the Bible tells me so."

That is the greatest truth of the Bible and the heart of what we believe as Christians. This truth is majestically set forth for us in Jesus' lament over the city of Jerusalem when

He said, "O, Jerusalem, Jerusalem, who kills the prophets and stones those who are sent to her! How often I wanted to gather your children together, the way a hen gathers her chicks under her wings, and you were unwilling" (Matt. 23:37).

The occasion for this statement was Jesus' last public appearance before His crucifixion. Jesus had offered Himself to Jerusalem and to the whole Jewish nation as their Messiah-King again and again. By miracles, by fulfilled prophecy, and by His preaching, He had declared Himself to be God's anointed Son. Salvation had been proclaimed to Jerusalem, but Jerusalem had refused the grace offered.

In rejecting God's Son, they were rejecting God Himself. Because of their rejection, God would withdraw His presence from the city and its Temple, leaving them desolate, empty, and alone. The result would be the total destruction of the Temple, Jerusalem, and nearly the whole Jewish nation.

Jesus could see all of this coming and knew that it could be averted if they would but recognize, acclaim, and follow Him as their Savior and King.

But they would not accept Him, so judgment was inevitable. There is no note of glee in what Jesus predicted. In deepest sorrow, He announced the impending judgment. This was a scene of sobs and tears. Heartbreak runs through every word as Jesus lamented over the city of Jerusalem. Note the beautiful analogy that He used to describe what He desired to do for His city and for the whole world. He said, "How often I wanted to gather your children together, the way a hen gathers her chicks under her wings" (Matt. 23:37).

If you are familiar with farm life, you know that a mother hen uses her wings to shelter and protect her brood. Let the night fall, let the wind begin to blow, let some danger threaten and the little ones rush instinctively to their mother's side, and she stretches out her wings and pulls them up close to her for safety. This is a picture of what Jesus desired to do with Jerusalem. He longed to reach out and put His arms as sheltering wings around her and draw her to Himself for safety and salvation.

This analogy presents the dominant message of the whole Bible—the grace of God and the compassion of Christ. Follow Jesus through all of His ministry and you will see Him reaching out again and again to draw all ages, all classes, all races of people unto Himself.

Three particular groups of people were and are still the objects of Jesus' affection. They are the smallest child, the biggest sinners, and His worst enemies. These three groups reveal to us the depth and the breadth of His great love.

Little Children

First, Jesus loves the smallest child. In the New Testament world, little children were considered of little importance. They certainly were not important enough to bother a teacher as great and as busy as Jesus. Therefore, when mothers began to bring their little ones to Jesus, desiring that He touch and bless them, the disciples intervened to prevent the children from coming. The disciples did not think that Jesus had time for such insignificant things.

When Jesus learned of this, He was angered and said to His disciples, "Let the children alone, and do not hinder them from coming to Me; for the kingdom of heaven belongs to such as these" (Matt. 19:14).

Jesus not only welcomed these children but also used them as models of the kind of faith and trust necessary for anyone to enter into the kingdom of God. We are always wanting children to come to Jesus like adults. He wants adults to come to Him as little children.

Little children, the weakest among us, were then and are still the objects of our Lord's love.

As a mother hen stretches out her wings to draw her little ones unto herself, so our Savior reaches out to draw the little ones unto Himself. They are the objects of His love not only because they are made in God's likeness and image but also because they have their whole lives ahead of them. If the little ones can be brought to Jesus, He not only can save their souls He can save their lives as well.

When D. L. Moody, the great evangelist, returned home from one of his revivals, a group of his men met him at the train. They asked, "Did you have a good revival meeting?" "No, not very good," replied Mr. Moody. "Were there many saved?" one of them asked. "No, only three and a half," Mr. Moody replied. "Do you mean three grown men and one little child?" one of them asked. "No, three little children and one grown man," was Mr. Moody's reply. "The man's life was half over."

When children come to Jesus, their whole lives are out ahead of them; and Christ can save children from many wasted years. As evangelist Gypsy Smith put it, "You save an old man and you save a unit; but save a boy and you save a multiplication table."

How old must a child be before he or she can be saved?

There can be no set age, of course, because not all children reach the age of understanding and moral and spiritual accountability at the same time. But a child can experience genuine salvation when he or she reaches the level of maturity at which he or she recognizes personal sin and comes to Christ under the convicting power of the Holy Spirit.

And when that time comes, children can and should be brought to Jesus. Parents, teach your children early about Christ, for they begin early to sin.

We sometimes sing in our church:

> Jesus loves the little children,
>   All the children of the world;
> Red and yellow, black and white,
>   They are precious in His sight.
> Jesus loves the little children of the world.

This is not only a beautiful song but is also a great truth: Jesus does love children, and He longs to see them brought to Him for salvation.

Big Sinners

Jesus not only loves the smallest child but also the biggest sinner. One of the criticisms most often made of Jesus by the religious leaders of His day was: "This man receiveth sinners, and eateth with them" (Luke 15:2, KJV). The word "receiveth" literally means "welcomes." Jesus opened wide the doors of His life and welcomed sinners in as His friends. Like a mother hen, He reached out and sought to draw them unto Himself.

Tax collectors like Matthew and Zaccheus, who were

hated and despised by their own people, found a friend in Jesus. Zaccheus was a Jewish "Uncle Tom." He was a son of Abraham who became a traitor to his own people and went to work for Rome as a tax collector. Zaccheus was a little man who had big problems. He had an identity problem, a value problem, a moral problem, and a sin problem. But in Jesus he found a friend who accepted him, saved him, and transformed him into a new man.

Prostitutes like Mary Magdalene and the woman at the well of Samaria found a friend in Jesus also. The woman at Samaria had been married and divorced so many times that she no longer bothered with wedding ceremonies. She just took up living with her latest lover. Instead of condeming her, as everyone else did and as she did herself, Jesus loved her and thus transformed her into a flaming evangelist.

Jesus never condemned anyone whom society had already condemned. Jesus condemned "obvious" goodness more than He did "obvious" badness. He did not come to tell people how bad they were. He came to tell them how great God is. In loving them and accepting them, Jesus was able to transform them.

We make a great mistake if we think the mercy of God is not extended to those who need it the most. The Bible declares, "God demonstrates His own love toward us, in that while we were yet sinners, Christ died for us" (Rom. 5:8). God did not love us in our righteousness or in our purity or in our innocence. He loved us when we hated Him, ignored Him, and rejected Him. Even the biggest of sinners is the object of God's love and Christ's compassion.

This means that you may have desecrated God's day, but still He loves you. You may have blasphemed His name, but still He loves you. You may have scoffed at His word, but still He loves you. You may have stolen His money, but still He loves you. You may have broken every one of His laws, but still He loves you.

So what was intended as a jibe by His critics has become Christ's crowning glory. He *does* welcome sinners as His friends. Jesus defended His acceptance of an association with sinners by saying, "It is not those who are healthy who need a physician, but those who are sick" (Mark 2:17). Well people do not need a doctor. Healthy people do not need a hospital. The sick need a physician, and sinners need the Savior. Jesus said, "I have come for those who need me the most."

Hugh Redwood tells of a woman in the dock district in London who came to a church women's meeting. She had been living with a Chinese man; by him she had had a baby, and she brought the baby with her. She liked the meeting, and she came back and back again. One day the vicar came to her. "I must ask you," he said, "not to come to this meeting again." The woman looked at him questioningly. "The other women," said the vicar, "say that they will stop coming if you continue to come." She looked at him with a poignant wistfulness. "Sir," she said, "I know I'm a sinner, but isn't there anywhere a sinner can go?" Fortunately, the Salvation Army found that woman, and she was reclaimed for Christ.

But her question still haunts us. Where can sinners go? Let me tell you where they can go. They can go to heaven. Jesus loves them and will receive them, and He has gone to prepare a place for them (John 14:1-6). There is nothing that we can do to keep God from loving us and reaching out to us.

So Jesus not only loves little children but also loves big sinners.

His Greatest Enemies

Perhaps the most amazing thing about God's love is that not only does He love the smallest child and the biggest sinner but He also loves His worst enemies. The very same people over whom He wept would soon be screaming, "Crucify Him! Crucify Him!" Jerusalem had stoned the prophets and had killed God's servants who had been sent to her by God; now she was rejecting God's own Son. The religious leaders are rejecting Jesus as God's incarnate in favor of the outward trappings of religion in which they had a vested interest. This is always the greatest danger of institutional religion. But in spite of their rejection and in spite of their demand for His crucifixion still, Jesus wept over them and longed to save them.

This scene depicts the breaking heart of God—even for those who spurn His love and will kill His Son. That's contrary to the kind of love most of us have. As long as people love us, we love them. As long as they speak well of us, we speak well of them. But beyond that, we show very little love or compassion. But God loves even those who reject Him and those who will crucify Jesus.

While in Hitler's prison, Martin Niemoller wrote: "It took me a long time to learn that God was not the enemy of my enemies. He is not even the enemy of His enemies." He is a God of love, and that love extends to those who oppose Him and hate Him the most.

God's love is unending and inexhaustible. In spite of our sin, in spite of our cruelty, in spite of our rejection, in spite of our unbelief, still He loves us.

Mike Burger, a newspaper columnist, wrote about a little boy who had a piece of chalk and who drew a valentine heart on the wall of the New York City library. Inside the chalked heart, he scrawled a delightful message "Billy Meyer loves everybody." If you will read the Bible with receptive eyes, you will see inscribed throughout its pages this message: "God loves everybody."

The psalmist spoke of the eternal and exhaustible love of God when he wrote, "When my father and my mother forsake me, then the Lord will take me up" (Ps. 27:10, KJV). The word *take* means "to gather." It is the same picture that we have here of Jesus longing to gather us unto Himself as a hen gathers her chickens unto herself.

Who are the last people on earth who would forsake us? Aren't they our own mothers and fathers? When no one else believes in us, trusts us, cares about us, or will help us, we can always count on them. But the Scriptures say that even when they let us down, God won't. There is one who loves us more than our own parents love us.

If that is true, we can safely say that if our husbands or our wives divorce us, the Lord will take us up. If the police arrest us, the Lord will take us up. If our bosses fire us, the Lord will take us up. If a jury convicts us, the Lord will take us up. If friends betray us, the Lord will take us up. If the judge sentences us, the Lord will take us up. Even if our mothers and fathers let us down, the Lord will take us up. There is nothing we can ever do to keep Him from loving us and reaching out to us.

The love of Jesus will not be silent. Though judgment is coming, He keeps saying, "How often would I . . . and ye would not" (KJV). That is the very heart of sin: the human will set against the will of God. Jesus would soon face death, but He assured His hearers that His death was not the end. He will come again in glory at the end of the age, and His coming will echo the acclamation of the crowds at His triumphal entry, "Blessed is He who comes in the name of the Lord" (Matt. 21:9).

He came the first time in His humility; He will return in glory. He came the first time to be crowned with thorns; He will come again to be crowned with the royal diadem. He came the first time to be crucified; He will return to be glorified.

Jerusalem will see her rejected King again when He comes in glory. Then on that day, all will acclaim Him as the One sent by the Lord and the One who loves all the world.

The late President Lyndon B. Johnson had inscribed on the doormat of his ranch home in Texas these words: "All the world is welcome here." I do not know that there will be doormats in heaven. But if there are, I feel confident that the words inscribed on them will be the same: "All the world is welcome here." That is the very heart of God's message to us through Christ today.

9

The Urgency of Now

One of the most misunderstood statements Jesus ever made was, "For the poor you always have with you" (John 12:8). Those words have been used to justify everything from the complete neglect of the poor to the extravagant and wasteful spending on ourselves of everything we have. But they were never intended to suggest a lack of benevolence or the extravagant and selfish use of our resources. They were intended, however, to teach us an important truth about life.

The occasion for this statement was a banquet given in honor of Jesus. The reason for the feast was to celebrate the raising of Lazarus from the dead.

The supper was held in the home of Simon the leper who had been cured by Jesus. Apparently, he was a relative or a close friend of Lazarus's family because Martha served the meal and Mary was present also.

This was one of those happy occasions that Jesus was so often a part of. It is interesting and remarkable how often Jesus was invited out by people during His earthly ministry; and it is more amazing that He went, especially since He knew the motives behind many of the invitations.

Apparently, Jesus loved warm, informal gatherings, family dinners, and lavish wedding feasts. He savored the satisfying late-night conversations that sort out the day and distil the experiences into wisdom.

At those ancient suppers, people did not sit in chairs at tables as we do. They reclined on the floor, leaning on one elbow with their feet stretched out behind them. While Jesus was so reclined, Mary did a most remarkable thing. She took a pint of very expensive imported ointment and began to anoint the feet of Jesus with it and then to wipe His feet with her long, flowing hair.

In all probability, it was a spontaneous expression of love and devotion to Jesus. It is likely that as Mary reclined at the feast and looked at her brother Lazarus, such joy and gratitude welled up in her heart for Jesus that she took the most precious thing she owned and gave it to Jesus. It was a spontaneous and generous expression of love. It was not for show or recognition but out of sincere gratitude. It was an act of worship in which she acknowledged Jesus as Lord.

All of this incensed Judas. He was angered and offended at Mary and at Jesus for what appeared to him to have been a great waste. Judas calculated the value of this ointment at three hundred pence. A pence was a day's wage for a laborer. So the pint of ointment was valued at a year's salary for a laborer. It was quite an expensive item, and Judas suggested that it could have been sold and the money given to the poor.

But don't be fooled by Judas's apparent concern for the poor. It was just a cover-up for his greed, covetousness, and dishonesty. Luke tells us that Judas was the treasurer of the apostles and that he was a thief. He was accustomed to pilfering from the moneybag.

If Mary had sold the ointment and put the money in the bag, it would have given him a chance to take some of it for himself. That's all he was thinking of. But he disguised his greed as concern for the poor.

That was the character of Judas. He was a practical-minded man with an eye for bucks. As the country song says, "He didn't even take time to smell the roses." He was the type who would sell 'em but never smell 'em.

Judas was the kind of man who knew the cost of everything and the value of nothing. Since Jesus is the Son of God, how could giving Him one's highest and best ever be a waste? The descendants of Judas are still with us. They speak out in opposition of anything beyond the bare necessities that is spent on Christ and His cause. In the name of conservatism, they cover up their own greed and selfishness. They just want to keep it all for themselves.

Jesus defended Mary by saying that she had been saving the oil for the day of His burial (John 12:7). Whether Mary knew it or not, we cannot be sure, but Jesus saw her act as anticipation of and a preparation for His death. He had a clear vision of the cross. What Mary did was in anticipation of and preparation for His coming crucifixion. Thus, Jesus lent His approval to this extravagant act and became party to it. Judas saw it as a waste, but Jesus saw it as an act of worship and approved.

At this point, Jesus said to Judas, "For the poor you always have with you; but you do not always have Me" (John 12:8). Jesus was saying, "To help the poor is something that can be done at anytime, for they will always be

around. But I will not always be around. The opportunity
to express the kind of love Mary has expressed to me will
soon be past."

In no way does this statement suggest that we should
neglect the poor. The poor need to be fed. To help them
is our duty. But it is not our only duty. We are also to
worship Christ, to honor Christ, and to love Christ. It is not
a matter of either/or; we should do both. The fact is that
those who love Christ the most will also do the most for the
poor. Caring for the poor is not optional. We are stewards
of what we have, not owners. But the Lord is to be honored
too. He is worthy of our highest and our best.

The primary teaching here is that some things must be
done while the opportunity is here. Some things can be
done at almost any time. Other things, however, can be
done only when the opportunity presents itself. The opportunity to express the kind of love that Mary felt would soon
be past. But the opportunity to help the poor would always
be present because they would always be present.

So, while Judas complained about wasted money, Jesus
cautioned about wasted opportunities. That's the real
waste of life. Wasted money can be reearned, but wasted
time and wasted opportunities can never be reclaimed.

The extravagance approved of by Jesus is a challenge to
us today to keep our priorities straight and to be keenly
aware of time. It reminds us to seize and to squeeze every
minute for the most that is in it.

There are some things which we can do almost any time,
and there are some things which we will never do unless we
grasp the chance to do them when the opportunity comes.
We are frequently seized with the desire to do something

which is fine and generous and big hearted. Often we put it off; we plan to do it tomorrow; the fine impulse is gone, and the thing is never done. Life is an uncertain thing. To help the poor was something that could be done anytime. To show the heart's devotion to Jesus had to be done before the cross of Calvary took Him into its cruel arms.

So the extravagance of Mary and of Jesus teachs us to do things now. For the chance often never comes again, and the failure to do them, especially the failure to express love, brings the bitterest remorse of all.

There are at least three things that must be done while the opportunity presents itself. If we delay, the chance to do them may never come again. The three things we should do now are: express our love, share our Lord, and yield our lives to Christ.

Express Love Now

Often we are moved to utter some word of thanks or praise or love to another person, but we put it off. It may be that we or the person we were thinking of will be gone from the earth suddenly and the word will never be spoken.

There is a tragic instance of how a man realized too late the things he had never said and done. Thomas Carlyle loved Jane Welch Carlyle, his wife, but he was a cross-grained, irritable creature; and he never made life happy for her. Unexpectedly, she died. A friend told of Carlyle's feelings when his wife died:

> He was looking through her papers, her notebooks, and journal; and old scenes came mercilessly back to him in the vistas of her mournful memory. In his long sleepless nights,

he recognized too late what she had felt and suffered under his childish irritabilities. His faults rose up in remorseless judgment, and as he had thought too little of them before, so he exaggerated them to himself in his helpless repentance . . . "Oh!" he said again and again, "if I could see her but once more, were it but for five minutes, to let her know that I always loved her through all of that. She never did know it. Never."

There is a time for doing and saying things; and when that time has passed, they can never be said and they can never be done. The realm of silence is great enough beyond the grave. Don't let it extend into the now by putting off too long the expression of your love. Perhaps you need to say to your wife, your husband, your parents, or your children again, "I love you." Don't wait until it is too late. Once the opportunity is gone, it is gone forever.

Several years ago Orville E. Kelly learned that he had lymphocytic lymphoma, a cancer of the lymph glands for which there is no established cure. He was given from six months to three years to live.

Like many cancer patients and persons with other life-threatening diseases, Orville Kelly gave way to despair. To him cancer meant death and death in a horrible manner. And like most people who are going to die, he went through identifiable stages of grief: denial and isolation, anger, bargaining for time, depression, and finally acceptance.

At first he spent most of his time alone, not talking to anyone not even reading or watching TV. He sat at home trying to deal with the idea that his children would grow up without him, that his wife would have to support the family without his help. Gloom hung over the household even though the word *cancer* was never mentioned and the children had not been told. Silence walled out most natural expressions of affection, anxiety, and grief.

Then one day a positive change occurred in Kelly's outlook. He decided that he didn't have to like death, but he didn't need to be terrified by it either. So he told his children of his illness and started concentrating on living instead of dying.

In time Orville Kelly founded Make Today Count(MTC), an organization devoted to improving the quality of life for the terminally ill and their families during their remaining time together.

MTC has become a nationwide organization and has helped thousands of Americans with life-threatening illnesses reconsider their priorities and choose what matters most. As a result, some have grown closer to their spouses and other family members; many have prepared for death in a positive way.

Deanna Edwards wrote a song for Make Today Count that expresses the truth which we need to remember:

> If I had just twenty-four hours for living,
> the things that don't matter
>   could wait.
> I'd play with the children,
>   hear all of their stories,
> I'd tell you I love you before it's
>   too late.

Listen! The poor we will have with us always. But we won't always have our loved ones with us. If we have something to say to them, we'd better say it now. Don't wait until it is too late.

Share a Witness Now

Another thing we need to do now is to share our faith. I am sometimes called by people who are concerned about the salvation of friends or relatives who are very, very old and very, very ill. When they ask if I will go and make sure of the person's salvation, I always think, *Why didn't you call sooner? Why did you wait until they were so old? So sick? Why did you wait until there is almost no hope?* The time to bear witness is now. The time to be concerned about the salvation of loved ones and friends is today. If we wait too long, we may be too late.

Bishop Phillip Brooks became ill and was so weak he would not see anyone. Robert Ingersol, an agnostic, heard Brooks was in this grave condition and visited him, "I do appreciate your seeing me. Why me when you have denied your friends this privilege?" The bishop looked at him, tearfully, "Mr. Ingersol, I know I shall see most of my friends after this life. This may be my last chance to talk with you about your destiny." Those who love Christ must see how imperative it is to introduce friends to Christ. This is still our choice and may be their last chance.

Paul urged believers to redeem the time because the days are evil (Eph. 5:16). The word *redeem* is a marketplace term that means "to buy up" or "to purchase." The word *time* means "opportunities." Paul was suggesting that we use every opportunity to its fullest. The only way we can save time in life is to spend it well. How you spend your time is more important than how you spend your money. Money mistakes can be corrected, but time is lost forever.

The steamship *Californian* passed only ten miles from the sinking *Titanic,* but a friend of its radio operator was playing with the set, and no messages were heard. When the "unsinkable" steamer struck an iceberg at 11:40 PM, April 15, 1912, 1,517 lives were lost. The *SS Carpathia* was a far greater distance from the sinking *Titanic* than was the *Californian.* But no one in the wireless room was playing with the set. The cries of distress were heard, and the *SS Carpathia* arrived in time to save several hundred lives. The *Californian,* only ten miles away, became aware of the tragic loss only after it was too late.

In these days of crises, we must not be caught playing at Christianity or playing with the gospel when people are perishing. We must seize every opportunity to share the gospel with others. The poor we will have with us always, but our lost friends and family members will not be here forever. If we want to win them to Christ, we had best do it today.

Make a Decision Now

In March, 1980, with age-old pomp and cermony, Archbishop Robert Alexander Kennedy Runcie M.C. was enthroned at Canterbury Cathedral as the 102 primate of all England and head of the world's sixty-five million Anglicans. Shortly thereafter, *Reader's Digest* published a selection of the archbishop's favorite prayers. One of them was entitled "On a Cathedral Clock" by Cannon Henry Twells. It goes like this:

When as a child, I laughed and wept,
    time crept.
When, as a youth, I waxed more bold,
    time strolled.
When I became a full-grown man,
    time ran.
When older still I daily grew,
    time flew.
Soon I shall find, in passing on,
    time gone.
Oh, Christ, will thou have saved me then?
Amen.

The crucial question of time and eternity is this: When Christ comes or when we go in death, will we be saved?

C. S. Lewis wrote, "Our future is what we are rushing into at a rate of sixty minutes an hour." We know that when a baby is born the birth certificate is a sentence of death. We live in a world where time keeps pressing its foot on the petal and death holds itself in readiness to jam on the brake! So whatever we intend to do for Christ we had best do now. The poor will be here always, but we won't always be here. We'd better do what we ought to do now while we can.

There is a proverb that says, "Hell is floored with good intentions and roofed with lost opportunities." Whatever decision we need to make for Christ, we should make it now. This may be the only opportunity we have to make it.

C. E. Matthews was the first director of evangelism for Texas Baptists. Once his twelve-year-old daughter came to him and asked for a pair of white knee socks. They were in style at the time, everyone else had a pair, and she felt that she must have a pair also. He surveyed the needs and his own resources and said no to her.

As children often do, she went to her mother and without telling her what her dad said she asked her for the socks. Her mother said yes.

Just a few weeks after that, Matthews stood beside the open casket of his little girl. She had died suddenly. As he looked at her still, lifeless body, he saw that she had on those white knee socks. He said, "I thought, *I'd give everything I've got if I had just said yes to her that day.*"

If you have persistently said no to Jesus Christ, the day will come when you stand before Him and you will say in your heart, "I'd give everything I've got if I had just said yes to Him that day."

Another time and another place—that's Satan's motto. But God says, Here and now. That's the challenge of Christ's extravagance. Decide for Christ today.

10

The Interruptions of Life

"All of my life I have been complaining about interruptions to my work," wrote a professor. "Now as I look back, I have discovered that my interruptions have been my work."

In a day when most of us are pressed by more demands than we can meet, we must learn to use the interruptions of life as well as the appointments of life for the glory of God and the good of others. Unless we do, we will live frustrated and ineffective lives.

Jesus is our example in how we are to do this. He lived His life on the tight timetable of God's will. Yet He was never too busy to help the needy. In fact, His sermons, His meals, His prayers, and even His rest were often interrupted by a barrage of questions, complaints, and requests for help.

No matter what the circumstances, Jesus was always gracious and accommodating. He was never irritated by interruptions. He looked upon them as opportunities to minister.

One example of how Jesus did this is in dealing with the Syrophoenician woman. Jesus had traveled into the region of Tyre and Sidon for some much needed seclusion and rest. But His fame was so widespread that He could not be hidden.

While He was resting in the home of a friend, a woman whose daughter was possessed by a demon came to Him for help. She was a Greek and a pagan by religion. By nationality she was a Phoenician of Syria. She fell at Jesus' feet and pleaded with Him to cast the demon out of her daughter.

Jesus responded, "Let the children first be filled: for it is not meet to take the children's bread, and to cast it unto the dogs" (Mark 7:27, KJV). In this statement Jesus interpreted His ministry. He had come first to the lost sheep of the house of Israel. His ministry was primarily to the Jews so they might in turn fulfill their mission of becoming a blessing to all nations through a worldwide proclamation of the gospel.

In this response, Jesus employed a common analogy from the eating practices of His day. In the first century world, people ate with their fingers. Knives and forks were not commonly used until around 1500 AD. Naturally, as people ate meat and other foods their fingers became greasy. Often a soft piece of bread was used to wipe the fingers clean, then it was tossed on the floor for the dogs to eat. In Jesus' analogy, the bread represents the Word of God. The children represent the Jewish nation. And the dogs represent the Gentiles. *Dog* was a common term of derision used to describe anyone who was not a Jew. At first glance, it appears that Jesus was calling the woman a dog and that He was saying that she and her people were excluded from His mission.

This is shocking! That kind of talk was unlike Jesus, but

very much like the Jewish pride of that day. The Jews had become sinfully exclusive and held all other races in contempt.

The woman was quick-witted however. Undaunted by Jesus' reply, she seized the seeming rebuff from His lips and turned it to her advantage. She said, "Yes, Lord: yet the dogs under the table eat of the children's crumbs" (v. 28, KJV). She gave assent to His estimation of her and drew her own conclusion. She said in essence, "I may be only a dog, but even a dog gets to eat the crumbs. All I'm asking for is a crumb of the blessings available to the Jews. Even a dog should get that."

Jesus obviously spoke these words with tongue in cheek, for He did not treat the woman as a dog. He treated her as a child and welcomed her into the family. The woman must have taken His remarks as He intended them, for she was not diverted by His seeming rebuff.

Her reply amazed Jesus. He said to her, "For this saying go thy way; the devil is gone out of thy daughter" (v. 29, KJV). And when the woman returned to her house she found her daughter healed. Jesus recognized in the woman's response an evidence of genuine faith; thus He healed her daughter. He healed her without going to her house. He healed her without even a command. He healed her in silence and at long distance.

This experience must be read with insight and spiritual perception. It teaches us much about our Lord and how He dealt with the interruptions of life. The Lord showed in this experience that in Him all social barriers are broken down and all racial privilege is nothing; all people of simple faith can approach Him at anytime. He was obviously delighted with this woman's response and stretched His mission so as to include her in the scope of it. God never seeks to save as few but as many as possible. This lady may very well be the first Gentile convert in Jesus' ministry. And this scene foreshadows the universal scope of the gospel.

This interruption of Jesus teaches us several important truths about Him and how He dealt with the interruptions of life.

No One Is Unimportant

First, there are no unimportant people to Christ. At first reading of this story, we might think differently. But don't be fooled by the fact that Jesus insinuated that the woman was a dog. He didn't mean that. It was only a test of her faith. He was obviously pleased with her response and treated her as a person of dignity and worth. He gladly broadened His ministry to include her in it.

Jesus clearly demonstrated what He consistently illustrated in His daily life: No people are unimportant people to God. Whenever any person came to Jesus, regardless of who they were, they were met with love, acceptance, and help. He ignored all artificial barriers and welcomed every one who came to Him.

The religion of the Jews in Jesus' day was exclusive, sinfully exclusive. But Jesus did not share that exclusiveness.

All sorts of people came to Jesus during His earthly ministry. Women, men, and little children came. The rich and the poor came. The elite and the outcast came. The insignificant and the influential came. But regardless of who they were and what their standing in society was, they were met with open arms. And if we will come to Him today, we will get the same kind of reception.

We may be unimportant to other people. There are some people who value others only for what they can get out of them. Still others feel that they are unimportant themselves. They lack an appropriate sense of self-worth. They suffer from an inferiority complex.

The starting point for both success and happiness in life is a healthy, positive, self-image. Our self-concepts are the core of our personalities. It affects every aspect of our behavior—our ability to learn; our capacity to grow and change; our choice of friends, mate, and career; and how we relate to other people. It is no exaggeration to say that a strong, positive self-image is the best possible preparation for success in life.

Poor self-image is generally revealed in a critical and jealous nature and in a breakdown of motivation. People who feel good about themselves usually feel good about others and have both the energy and the incentive necessary to go at life enthusiastically.

Where does poor self-image come from? Possibly the most significant cause of poor self-image is that personal ability, intelligence, and future have been questioned repeatedly by parents, teachers, friends, and others in authority. While no one can make us feel inferior without our permission, many people subconsciously believe what others say to them and about them.

Still other people have an inferiority complex because they compare themselves with other people in a most unrealistic and unfair manner. We cannot help but make comparisons in life; but if those comparisons are unrealistic and unfair, the result can be devastating to our own abilities, potential, and talents.

The best way to overcome an inferiorty complex and to develop good positive self-image is to see ourselves as God sees us. I once read a bumper sticker that said, "God loves you whether you like it or not." To see ourselves as God sees us should change our lives altogether. He loves and values each of us. He thought we were worth dying for. We may be unimportant to others and we may feel unimportant about ourselves, but we are not unimportant to Him.

Some people are so exclusive and narrow-minded that their ears touch each other. But love is never exclusive. It always reaches out to include. For this reason, the church must never see itself as an extension of country club exclusiveness. We must always say to the poor, Come. We say to the uneducated, Come. We say to the unemployed, Come. We say to the alcoholic and to the ex-convict, Come. We say to the blacks, Come. We say to the browns and the yellows, Come. We say to all men everywhere, Come. We say in words of Jesus, "Whosoever will, let him [come and drink of] the water of life freely" (Rev. 22:17). It is a sad day when the church begins to see itself as a select society of splendid saints.

Jesus' reaction to this interruption indicates that all people are important to God. And our reaction to life's interruptions show how we value people also.

Nothing Is Impossible

Second, there are no impossible problems with Jesus; there is no difficulty beyond His help. The Syrophoenician woman's daughter had a demon. There were no doctors of demons in her city. She was distraught at her daughter's illness and sought healing from the only source available. Like this woman, we must face our need and our helplessness or we will never get any help. We must frankly face our desperate need of what only Christ can give.

There are no problems beyond the Savior's help. I see people come to Jesus with every conceivable need. They come with broken hearts, broken homes, broken health, broken dreams, broken spirits, broken reputations, broken careers, broken vows, and broken lives; and Jesus helps them to put things back together again. I know of no problem that is beyond His redemption.

The biggest problem we face is that of sin. The message of the gospel is that all our faults and inadequacies, failings, and sins are already recognized by God, and still He loves us. While we were yet sinners, Christ died for us. "The wages of sin is death, but the free gift of God is eternal life in Christ Jesus our Lord" (Rom. 6:23). He is the answer to the greatest problem we face, and He is the answer to all other problems also.

But we must face our need and come to Him with it. As this woman came, we must come. As she knelt in humility, so we must humble ourselves. As she asked for help, so we must ask for help. When we do, we have this promise, "Him that cometh to me I will in no wise cast out" (John 6:37, KJV).

Like this woman, we must recognize who Jesus is, believe He will help us, come to Him, and ask for His help. When we do that, we will discover that no problem in our lives is beyond His help.

When I was a boy we sang a chorus that goes like this:

Are there any rivers that seem to be uncrossable?
Are there any mountains you cannot tunnel through?
God specializes in things that seem impossible,
He knows a thousand ways to make a way for you.

There are no unimportant people, and there are no impossible problems with our Lord. Jesus' response to this interruption teaches us this.

Call Out in Faith

Third, Jesus always responds to the plea of faith. The most remarkable thing about this story apart from our Lord's power is the faith of the Phoenician lady. She believed and would not be denied. When Jesus saw her persistence in asking, her humble trust, her genuine faith, He had to respond to her in spite of the fact that she interrupted His rest.

What is faith? It is not some mysterious quality that cannot be understood. It is knowing who Jesus is, believing that He loves and cares and will help, and asking Him to do so. Faith is believing the promises of God and acting upon them.

Faith is never passive. It is never merely intellectual. It is always dynamic and active. Faith is confident assurance in God. The Scriptures say, "Without faith it is impossible to please Him; for he that cometh to God must believe that He is, and that He is a rewarder of them that diligently seek him" (Heb. 11:6, KJV). We can do a lot of things without faith. We can earn livings without faith. We can build businesses without faith. We can even become millionaires without faith. But we cannot come to God and we cannot please God without faith.

Faith is recognizing Jesus as the Savior, the Son of God, believing in His love and His compassion and His power, falling on our knees before Him as the Phoenician woman did, and crying out, "Lord, help me." If we have enough faith to do that, He will help us.

I used to pray, "Lord, give me more faith." Then I stopped wasting God's time and my own time. I discovered that all I needed was a pinch of faith. Didn't Jesus say, "If you have the faith of a grain of mustard see, you can say to a mountain, 'Be thou moved' and the mountain will be moved?" Jesus said that it takes only a small amount of faith to do miraculous things. You and I have that much faith, don't we? What we need to do then is use the faith that we have. Faith is like anything else; it is not how much of it you have but what you do with what you have that matters.

Faith is like intelligence. The important thing about intelligence is not how much we have but what we do with what we have. Faith is like money. The important thing about money is not how much we have but what we do with what we have. Faith is like talent. What matters is not how much ability we have but what we do with what we have. Faith is like time. What matters is not how much time we have but what we do with the time that we have. And what matters to God is not how much faith we have but what we do with the faith that we have.

Do you want your sins forgiven? Then ask Him. He will do it. Do you want strength for life? Then ask Him. He will give it to you. Do you want guidance and direction for your life? Then ask Him. He will guide and direct you. Do you want help for your home? In your school work? In your career? Then ask Him. He will help you.

If you have enough faith to ask, He cannot say no to the plea of faith. Jesus' response to the Phoenician woman's interruption makes it clear. But you must come as she came. You must humble yourself as she humbled herself. And you must ask as she asked. If you will say to him, "Lord, help me," He will do it, and He will do it today.

On one occasion when the presidential party of Thomas Jefferson was traveling by horseback, they had to cross a swollen stream. A man standing by the stream asked the president for a ride to the opposite shore. Jefferson lifted the man onto his horse, carried him across, and set him down. Someone in the group asked the man why he chose the president. "I didn't know it was the president," he replied. "Some faces have yes written on them, and others have no. The president has a yes face.

Jesus has a yes face. That is the reason so many people come to Him for help. And He is the same yesterday, today, and forever. He still has a yes on His face, and if you will come to Him, He will help you now.

After seeing how Jesus dealt with the interruptions of life, my prayer for you and for me is: "Lord, bless us in the interruptions of life as well as in the appointments of life. Help us to be like Jesus and use both of them for Your glory and the good of others."

11

Give What You Have

These two facts are equally true: Man does not live by bread alone, and neither does he live without bread. Jesus recognized both of these needs. By the miracle of feeding the multitudes, He not only declared Himself to be the Bread of life for the souls of men, He also provided bread for the bodies of men.

This miracle occurred in the region of Decapolis on the eastern shores of the Sea of Galilee (Mark 8:1-9). As Jesus preached and taught, the crowds grew larger and larger until there was such a vast multitude that a kind of camp-meeting atmosphere prevailed. Many had brought their lunch baskets, so they could stay as long as possible.

For three days the people stayed, sleeping on the ground at night and eagerly pressing around Jesus, the great wonder-worker, by day. Jesus was deeply touched by the sight of the multitudes composed largely of Gentiles. To Jesus it was symbolic of the wider conquest of the kingdom in the future. During the three days, naturally, the people exhausted their supply of food; yet they would not leave. These Gentiles had never witnessed things like this and were charmed beyond words by Jesus.

But Jesus expressed concern to His disciples about how to care for the crowd. He did not want to send them away hungry because many of them had traveled great distances and could not stand the long journey home without food. He wanted to know if His disciples knew of any way to feed them.

The apostles probably remembered that Jesus had fed five thousand in Galilee by multiplying five loaves and two small fish. Would He feed this multitude the same way?

They obviously didn't think so, for they responded that there was not enough food to feed such a crowd and that they did not know where to get enough. They were in the open country, and there was no place to secure that much food. So they presented Jesus with a picture of helplessness and hopelessness. They realized the problem, but their resources were inadequate.

Jesus then asked, "How many loaves have ye?" (v. 5, KJV). They told Him that they had only seven loaves. Jesus took the seven loaves, thanked God for them, and gave them to His disciples to distribute among the multitude. Someone then found a few small fish, so Jesus blessed them and commanded that they be given to the multitude also. To the astonishment of everyone, the crowd of over four thousand had been fed and seven baskets full of food were left over.

Several truths may be learned from this experience. For one thing, Jesus was compassionate. Confront Jesus with a lost soul or a tired body and His first instinct was to help. That is not true of all religious leaders. Many evangelists are concerned about getting a crowd, fleecing the crowd, and manipulating the crowd, but beyond that they could not care less about them. But Jesus cared about the needs of His crowd, even on their way home.

This experience also teaches us that Jesus was consistent. He not only taught us to thank God for our daily bread but also gave thanks Himself.

We can also learn that Jesus was cooperative—He used people in His work. Jesus multiplied the loaves and fish, but He used His disciples as distributors. This is most often the way of God. He walks to His mission on human feet. He speaks His message through human lips. And He feeds the hungry through human hands. What God does, He usually does in cooperation with people.

But the primary lesson that we learn from this miracle is that Jesus was the Master over circumstances. He is here revealed as the Master of multiplication who takes what we bring to Him and multiplies it to meet the needs of multitudes.

The spiritual significance of this experience as told by John is that Jesus is the Bread of life. He alone is able to satisfy the deepest hunger of the human spirit.

What I want to focus on here is the miracle-working power of our Savior. He can take our little and multiply it into a lot just as He did two thousand years ago. Focus on the problem that Jesus presented, the response of His disciples, and finally the solution that Jesus offered.

The problem was that the vast throng of four thousand people did not have anything to eat. When Jesus had pity on the crowd and wished to feed them, the disciples immediately pointed out the practical difficulty. They were in the open countryside, and there was no place for miles around where food could be obtained.

Notice that the disciples were focusing on what they did not have and what they could not do. They were focusing on failure and dwelling on the negative. What a tragic thing to do! Yet that is exactly what many people do when they are confronted with a difficulty.

Some people walk around like a cruise director on the *Titanic,* expecting to ship to sink at any minute. They are like the boy who came home from school and told his father, "Dad, I think I failed my arithmetic test today." The father, desiring to teach the boy to be a positive thinker said, "Son, think positive." The boy responded, "All right, I'm positive I failed my arithmetic test." Many people are like that; they are positively negative.

What makes negativism so tragic is that most of the barriers in life are mental. If we think a thing can't be done, we usually don't even try. And if we do try, we give it a half-hearted effort. If we focus on what we don't have rather on what we do have, we end up doing little or nothing. If everyone thought that way, many of the world's greatest accomplishments would never have come to pass.

Don't forget that Shakespeare had no typewriter; Galileo had no computer; and David decked Goliath without the help of Howard Cosell.

Christ responded to His disciples' negative statement by ignoring it. He asked instead, "How many loaves have ye?" It was as if Jesus was saying, "I'm not interested in what you don't have. Tell me what you do have. Give it to me! Let's see what I can do with it." When they complied, Jesus multiplied their little into a lot. He took their insufficiency and made it sufficient.

The disciples grossly overestimated their poverty. They

failed to look at their resources. They felt that they had
nothing, but they had Jesus and that was enough. In His
hands, what they had become more than adequate.

The great truth of this miracle is that we need to stop
thinking about and dwelling on what we don't have. We
need to take what we have, put it in the hands of Jesus, and
let Him multiply it.

There are at least three areas of life where this truth
needs to be applied. It needs to be applied to our abilities,
our resources, and our witness.

Give Him Your Talents

Herschel Hobbs in his book *The Gospel of Giving* tells
about a young serviceman who accepted the call to be a
medical missionary. He faced a long, hard road of preparation. In one of his letters to Hobbs, the young man made
one of the most poignant statements I have ever read. He
said, "I have so little in myself, and my abilities need great
development, but I know that God has never asked a man
to do anything that was too hard for him to accomplish. I
intend to do all that I can by every possible means, to serve
Him." Then he added these words, "If I do what I can, God
will do what I can't."

Twelve words—no more, no less—but they sum up the
message of this miracle. The real question in life is, Will
you do what you can? Our biggest problem is that we often
don't do what we can. We are like a former staff member
who called me recently. I asked, "How are you doing?" He
replied, "I am doing great. I am working with a pastor who
doesn't do anything, and I'm helping him."

There are a lot of people around who aren't doing anything, and there are a lot of others who are helping them. Jesus didn't make bread out of nothing. Jesus didn't multiply nothing and get fish. He did take seven loaves and a few fish and multiply them. It is difficult for God to bless our nothingness. We need to get busy and go to work for God. We can give Him the labor, the abilities, the talents that we have and He can multiply and bless them.

This has been true of all of God's servants who have been honored to accomplish great things for His cause. They have put what they had into His hands, and He has multiplied it to meet the emergency. All of them were painfully aware of their weaknesses, inadequacies, and deficiencies. But they gave themselves to God. I wish that all of us would put what we have in His hands and let Him do the rest. Christ is as mighty as ever, and what is needed is for us to give ourselves to Him as did His servants in the past.

Moses is a case in point. Moses was a timid, stammering shepherd with a tremendous inferiority complex. When God called Moses to lead the children of Israel out of Egyptian bondage, he had a multitude of reasons as to why he was not the man for the job. To convince the hesitant Moses of His great power, God asked, "What is that in your hand?" (Ex. 4:2). It was Moses' shepherd's staff. The Lord told him to throw it on the ground. As he did, it turned into a slithering snake. Then the Lord said to pick it up again. As Moses reached down and picked up the snake, it turned into a shepherd's staff again. If God were able to turn a shepherd's staff into a snake and then turn it back into a staff, surely He could turn the weak, inadequate Moses into a strong servant. That's exactly what He did.

God's question to Moses and Jesus' question to the disci-

ples are also His questions to us: "What is that in your
hand?" "How many loaves have ye?" Give them to the
Lord, and He will use them. What He did with Moses in the
Old Testament and what He did in Decapolis two thousand
years ago, He can still do today. He is the Master of multiplication.

So don't talk about the ability you don't have. Concen-
trate on what abilities you do have. Whatever they are, put
them in the hands of Jesus and see what He can do with
them. It is not ability but availability and dependability that
God is really looking for anyhow. So give your talents, no
matter how meager, to Jesus; He can multiply your effec-
tiveness.

Give Him Your Tithe

We should not only give Him our abilities but also our
resources. He can multiply them also. Mother Teresa of
Calcutta, India, has become an international symbol of
faith and real success. Once she had a dream. She told her
superiors, "I have three pennies and a dream from God to
build an orphanage."

"Mother Teresa," her superiors chided, "you cannot
build an orphanage with three pennies. With three pennies
you can't do anything."

"I know," she said smiling, "but with God and three
pennies I can do anything!"

In Alexandria, Louisiana, is one of the most beautiful
auditoriums in the south. For years the church worshiped
in an inadequate educational building. The adult membership spoke of the need of a place of worship, but always
they spoke of debt and of the large sum of money involved.

Finally after about fifteen years, a miracle happened. One Sunday night, Mrs. Lena David talked with her Intermediate Training Union about the need for an auditorium costing many thousands of dollars. At the close of her remarks, someone suggested that they take an offering with which to start a building fund. They did and received something like $3.56. This was turned over to the pastor who announced the sum in the church bulletin as the beginning of the building fund. A bank president of the congregation saw the article and mailed a sizable check to the church. Others took up the challenge. Today on the corner of Fourth and Jackson stands "The church in the heart of the city, in the heart of the state, for the hearts of the people."

Some people gave the little that they had, and God multiplied it into enough to meet needs. Some people talk about what they would give to God if they had a million dollars. God is not interested in what we would do if we had a million dollars. What He is interested in what we are going to do with the fifteen- to eighteen-thousand-dollar salary that we are making right now? If we are not faithful in the little things of life, there is no reason to believe that we would be faithful with the big things of life. If we don't give generously out of what we have, there is no reason to believe that we would give generously out of what we might get.

If our Lord could multiply seven loaves and a few fish into a meal for a multitude of four thousand people, surely He can multiply our small gifts also. If we give what we can, God will bless it.

Give Him Your Testimony

David Ben-Gurion, former prime minister of Israel, was asked what it would take to establish a new nation. He laughed and replied, "All I need starts with the letter *A*— *A* lot of planes, *A* lot of guns, *A* lot of money, *A* lot of men."

We, too, could say that all we need to expand Christ's kingdom starts with the letter *A*—*A* lot of love, *A* lot of prayer, *A* lot of dedication, and *A* few witnesses.

Some people talk about how they would serve the Lord if they just knew the Bible better, if they were seminary trained, if they could quote more Scripture. But God is not interested in what we don't know. He's interested in what we're doing with what we do know. We already know enough gospel to save the whole world. Our problem is not ignorance but indifference. If we would just share with others, our own testimony of Christ's working in our lives He could use that mightily.

Have you ever wondered where the vast crowd that Jesus fed came from? It was a tremendous crowd of over four thousand people. No doubt the healing of the deaf man, recorded in the previous chapter of Mark's Gospel, inspired some of it and helped to arouse the large multitude. But if you really want to know where they came from go back to Mark 5 and read about Jesus' healing the Gadarene demoniac. That wild man who lived among the tombs was made whole by Jesus. Then Jesus told him to go back to his people and tell them what great things the Lord had done for him. He did just that, and the whole country was caught up with what the Lord could do (Mark 5:19-20). That's where the crowd came from.

All this happened before the days of television. Nobody filmed Jesus' healing the demoniac and showed it on the ten o'clock news. It wasn't reported in the headlines of the local *Decapolis Times.* It wasn't carried as a news release over the local radio stations of that day. That healed man just began telling everybody what God had done for him. The people who heard him were so moved by his testimony that, when Jesus came back to that region, the whole countryside emptied out to see Him and to hear Him for themselves. They came basically because of the witness of one man.

Here we have a glimpse of what the witness of one person can do for Christ. No doubt there were people in the crowd that day who came to Christ and found new life because of the witness of that one man. Don't ever underestimate the importance of one person telling another what Christ has done.

Has He saved you? Has He forgiven you? Is there peace in your heart? Do you have the hope of heaven? Are you unafraid of dying? Do you know of His abiding presence? What has Jesus done for you? Tell somebody else. Forget the fact that you can't quote yards of Scripture, you don't teach a Sunday School class, or you haven't been to the seminary. Stop worrying about what you don't know and what you don't have, and start sharing what you do know with whatever ability you do have.

If you put what you have into the hands of Jesus, He can multiply it into a great and wonderful thing. The message of this miracle is that the Master who can take seven loaves and a few fish and multiply them into a meal for a multitude can also take our talents or our tithes or testimonies and multiply them so they bless great multitudes also.

An interesting fact about that experience is that it all occurred in Decapolis, which was largely inhabited by Gentiles. Earlier in Mark, Jesus had performed a miracle by feeding five thousand people. But at that time He was on the western shores of the Sea of Galilee, and His audience was largely Jewish. Now He was on the eastern shores of the Sea of Galilee, and His audience was largely made up of Gentiles. In both instances, He used the same miraculous power to provide bread.

When we put these two stories together, they suggest that Jesus came to satisfy the hunger of the Jews and the Gentiles alike. We see in Him the God who opens His hand and satisfies the desire of every living thing.

The feeding of the five thousand is understood as an invitation to the Jewish people to fellowship and to share Jesus' life. The feeding of the four thousand is understood as Jesus' inclusion of the Gentiles equally in full fellowship and in the sharing of His life. The Jews and the Gentiles were both provided for in Christ Jesus.

There are two great truths in that miracle: Jesus satisfies our needs, and He multiplies our potential. So in bringing what you have to Christ, don't forget to bring yourself. He wants both.

12

The Magnetism of the Cross

I sat one night in a dimly lit mission on the island of Trinidad in the West Indies. The congregation was composed chiefly of the black descendants of slaves who had been brought over from Africa years ago. The young man who was giving his testimony at that moment was the son of Hindu parents from India who had come there as merchants. I was attending the service with several missionaries.

As I looked around at the congregation my first thought was: *Isn't it strange that a Jewish carpenter dying on a Roman cross in the first century could have such an appeal to all of these varied races, classes, and nationalities?* But on second thought I said to myself, *No! No, it isn't surprising at all. This is exactly as Jesus said it would be, for He prophesied,* "And I, if I be lifted up from the earth, will draw all men to Myself" (John 12:32).

Then I realized for the first time in my life that I was in the midst of fulfilled prophecy. The Bible is full of prophecy. Some of it was fulfilled centuries ago, and some of it is yet to be fulfilled. But some Bible prophecy is being fulfilled in our very midst. This prophecy of Jesus is one of them.

Jesus said that, as a result of being lifted up from the earth on His cross, He would have a universal and an irresistible appeal, a magnetism. Men and women and boys and girls of all races, classes, nationalities, and religions would be drawn to Him. That cross would become His throne. Jesus knew that people might listen to His words and doubt them. They might see His miracles and question them. They might receive His gifts and soon forget them. But they would never be able to forget His crucifixion. It would give to Him an irresistible and universal magnetism.

This is amazing! The ghastly scene of a man dying on a cross as a common criminal, in agony and naked, should repulse people. Instead, it has become the magnet of God to touch human hearts everywhere and draw people to Jesus.

Why is this so? What is there about the cross that gives it such an appeal? Such magnetism today?

The Magnetism of Love

From the beginning of His ministry, Jesus enjoyed immense popularity. Wherever He went, crowds thronged to Him. All kinds of people, strong men, little children, and even sinners were attracted to Him.

What was it about Jesus that attracted people? It was Jesus' genuine love for them. It was the fact that He was a friend to sinners and was even willing to fellowship with them (Luke 15:1-2).

Today that love still has a magnetic appeal. But as winsome, as charming, as appealing as Jesus was in the flesh, the cross is still the noblest, most wonderful manifestation of God's love that the world has ever seen (John 3:16). It is the supreme expression of God's love and thus His magnetism to draw men unto Himself.

Where can we go to see the love of God today? We do not see it in the sun or the stars or the moon. We do not see it in nature. These all speak to us of the glory of God, the majesty of God, the power of God, and the intelligence of God. But there is nothing in the range of the telescope or the microscope that speaks to us of the love of God.

Walk, if you will, in the forest on a beautiful spring day. See the sunlight as it filters through the leaves of the trees, and listen to the wind as it whispers through their branches. And as you do you may say in your heart, *Here is an expression of the love of God.* But stay there awhile, and the sunlight and the breezes will turn into a summer storm. The heavens will roll with thunder, and lightning will rip across the sky; in those moments, I ask you, Where is the love of God now?

Or walk along the beaches of our coast as I love to do. Feel the warm gulf breeze in your face and feel the sand as it squeezes between your toes. Listen to the surf as it gently splashes against the shore. As you do, you might think, *Here is an evidence of the love of God.* But stay at the beach long enough and the cool breezes will become a howling gale. The gentle surf will become devastating surf. And hurricane winds will lash out in destruction everywhere. I ask you then, Where is the love of God?

Or you may look into the innocent face of a little baby and say, "Surely here the love of God is manifest." But go and visit the children's ward of a hospital in one of our major cities. There you will see the bodies of precious little children twisted and deformed by disease. As you see them in their agony, I ask you, Where is the love of God now?

The only place we can see the love of God in all of its glory and splendor is in the cross of Calvary. Herein is love! There could be no greater love than that Christ should lay down His life for us. Paul declared:

> For while we were still helpless, at the right time Christ died for the ungodly. For one will hardly die for a righteous man; though perhaps for the good man someone would dare even to die. But God demonstrates His own love toward us, in that while we were yet sinners, Christ died for us (Rom. 5:6-8).

The word *helpless* means that we are powerless to save ourselves. People do many things for themselves. We can build a submarine that will sail around the world under water. We have built a satellite to transmit messages around the globe in seconds. But there is one thing we can never do for ourselves: we can never save ourselves. We are completely and totally dependent upon God for salvation.

He has shown us His love and salvation in the cross and that's why it has such an appeal to people.

The Magnetism of Forgiveness

Another reason people have always been drawn to the cross of Christ and are still drawn to it is that they find in it forgiveness for their sins.

In a lonely cemetery in New York City is a grave with one word written on it: Forgiven. There is no name, no date of birth or death, no eulogy—just the word *Forgiven.* I personally would rather have that word written over me in eternity than any other word I know.

The Bible is filled with marvelous promises of God's full

and complete forgiveness. Isaiah wrote, "I, even I, am the one who wipes out your transgressions for My own sake;/ And I will not remember your sins" (Isa. 43:25). This is the only thing in the Bible which God is ever represented as forgetting. It is the one thing which we would most like for Him to forget.

David declared out of the depths of his own sin and shame: "I acknowledged my sin to Thee,/And my iniquity I did not hide;/I said, 'I will confess my transgressions to the Lord';/And Thou didst forgive the guilt of my sin" (Ps. 32:5).

How is such forgiveness possible? It has been made possible to us through the crucifixion of Christ. When Jesus died on the cross, He satisfied the just demands of God's holy judgment of sin (1 John 2:2). So on Calvary, what the justice of God demanded the love of God provided. The blood of Christ that was shed there cleanses us from all our sin (1 John 1:7; Rev. 5:7-9).

Because He knew that He would pay our debt on the cross, Jesus was able to offer forgiveness to all who sought it during His earthly ministry. To the repentant thief on the cross who was crucified next to Him, Jesus said, you are forgiven.

To Paul, the worst of sinners, Jesus said, You are forgiven.

To the woman caught in the very act of adultery, Jesus said, You are forgiven.

To Zaccheus, the greedy, money-grabbing tax collector, Jesus said, You are forgiven.

To the woman at the well in Samaria who had been

married and divorced five times and was now living with a
man she was not married to, Jesus said, You are forgiven.

To the paralyzed man whose muscles were twisted into
knots by guilt over his past sins, Jesus said, You are forgiven.

To the bloodthirsty crowd and the calloused soldiers
who crucified Him, Jesus cried, "Father, forgive them"
(Luke 23:34).

To Peter, one of his closest friends and one of his most
trusted disciples who denied Him during his trial, He said,
You are forgiven.

And to you and me, the Lord offers the same full and free
pardon of our sins. Two verses tell us exactly what we must
do to experience God's forgiveness. First, we must confess
our sins (1 John 1:9). Then we must turn away from our sin
and put our faith in Christ (Acts 3:19). So we must own and
then disown our sins. When we do these two things, God
can be trusted to forgive us of our sin and to cleanse us
from all unrighteousness.

Because people find in the cross of Jesus the complete
forgiveness of God, they are drawn to Him.

The Magnetism of Victory

Before Jesus spoke of His magnetic appeal from the
cross, He said, "Now judgment is upon this world; now the
ruler of this world shall be cast out" (John 12:31).

Jesus saw the cross as a contest between good and evil,
God and Satan, two rulers contending for world supremacy. But He also saw Satan as losing. He would be cast down
in defeat. The cross was the crisis point in the history of the
human race. There the prince of this world, Satan, con-

tended with Jesus Christ for the ultimate victory over people. But Christ prevailed, and the cross has become the symbol of victory for time and eternity. People have always seen in the cross the ultimate conquest of evil and triumph of good, and that's why they have been drawn to it.

After Napoleon was defeated at Waterloo, he was exiled on the island of Saint Helena. One day he was pouring over a map of Europe that had the British Isles outlined in red. He said to a companion, "Do you see that red spot? Were it not for that one red spot I'd have conquered the world."

Satan is saying the same thing today. Were it not for the red spot of Calvary in the history of the world, the victory over humanity would have been Satan's. But thanks be to God, the victory is ours through the Lord Jesus Christ. We now have victory over sin, over temptation, and over death because of Jesus' victory on the cross.

I recently buried a beautiful fourteen-year-old girl, Kara Chambers. She had fought and lost a long, grueling battle with cancer. In her Bible I found this inscription, "The way of the cross may not be easy, but it is the way home." Kara was right. The way of the cross is the way to love; it is the way to forgiveness; it is the way to victory; and it is the way home. That's why it has such a magnetic appeal today.